RIGHT BEHIND YOU

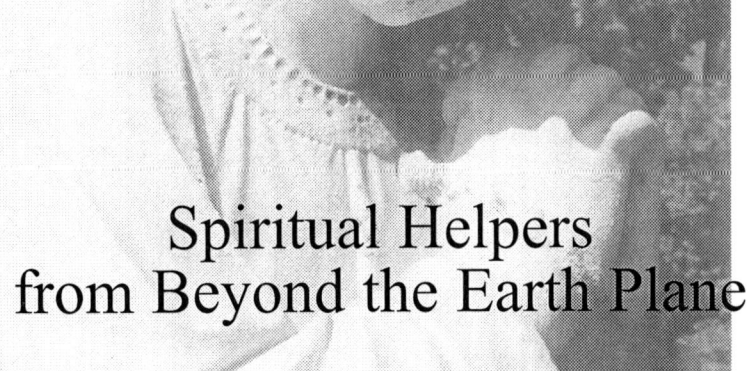

Spiritual Helpers
from Beyond the Earth Plane

By PJ Langhoff

Right Behind You, Spiritual Helpers from Beyond the Earth Plane is an original publication and this is the first time it has appeared in print form.

A print-on-demand publication

© 2006 by PJ Langhoff
Cover art and photography by PJ Langhoff

ISBN 978-1-4116-8443-0

For more information, write the author at the address listed at the end of this publication.

Printed in the U.S.A.

For my Family,
Both here on Earth and in Spirit,
and
To my Spirit Guides and Guardian Angels who
so lovingly guide everything that I do
while I visit this crazy plane of existence…

My religion consists of a humble admiration of
the illimitable superior spirit who reveals himself
in the slight details we are able to perceive
with our frail and feeble mind.

– Albert Einstein

TABLE OF CONTENTS

SPIRIT PHOTOGRAPHY

The photos on the following pages are meant to illustrate possible ways that Spirit makes itself known to us. Spirit photography is certainly not a new phenomenon, and there are many skeptics who discount its existence. Here are some examples for you to ponder...

(right) This photograph was taken in 1980 just prior to the author appearing on stage in a community play. Notice the orb of light just above her head. While some people may contend that the orb is created by dust particles, one seeks explanation for the fact that none of the other photographs were affected by this phenomenon.

The lower right part of this photo from 1998 shows a filmy white rotating mass leaving an oblong trail. There was nothing that would have created this effect on or near the camera at the time of the photo. Photo was taken at the location where a ghostly hand apparition appeared to the author.

The misty apparitions in the above photograph appeared around the author and her dog in the early 1980's in her apartment in Chicago, Illinois. If one looks closely, the distinctive outline of at least two, possibly three angels, wings included, may be seen. This visit occurred prior to the author's angelic warning not long before her apartment was vandalized. The warning given by her Angel or Spirit Guide prevented the author from being present at the time of a robbery, possibly saving her life. The photograph was taken by a friend visiting the author at that time.

(left) Taken in 1979 in a cemetery in the city of Philadelphia Pennsylvania, near a grave. There was a commemorative civil war ceremony occurring nearby at the time. The figure in the foreground was not visually present during the capturing of the ceremony on film. From the viewer's vantage point, the mist appears to be a deceased civil war veteran who we can imagine as wearing a hat from that time period. The photo was taken by the author, then aged 18.

How many will listen to the truth when you tell them?

– *Old Yiddish Proverb*

OUR SPIRITUAL PATH

The stories contained within this book are true and actual memories and events that transpired during my life, and are told as I remember them. The names of others appearing in this book have been changed to protect their privacy.

It is my hope that those reading these stories will come to understand in greater detail or perhaps for the first time, the myriad of ways in which Spirit connects with the living. Through this process, Spirit joins with each one of us individually, in a manner in which only we can understand. In its own way, Spirit moves us, guides us, teaches and protects, and reaches out to all in ways that transform us for the rest of our lives.

Despite the religious beliefs a person has, eventually Spirit finds a way to connect with us all, using a method that speaks uniquely to each. That is why no two stories about Angel encounters or Spiritual encounters are ever the same. Despite this, throughout history, a common thread has been woven proving beyond a shadow of a doubt that there is something larger out there, beyond the three-dimensional plane in which we live, known as our universe. It is only when we open ourselves up to receive the blessings of Spirit that we can become truly alive, as seekers and transformers, and not merely as beings walking aimlessly about on earth.

People who have experienced small miracles, near death experiences, unexplained phenomenon, ghostly encounters, and other paranormal experiences will be the first to admit that there is "something" going on outside of ourselves that perhaps at this time cannot be explained. That something is the Spiritual dimension and it is very much alive and willing to communicate with us. We just have to be open to receive the information that is designed to help us succeed on our life journey.

Through my personal experiences, I have learned many important lessons. Many of these were embarrassing, humiliating, and often immensely complex. Some lessons challenged me beyond what I ever thought I could physically or emotionally endure. I have been financially, emotionally and spiritually destitute many times over the course of my life. I have suffered a great deal of grief both at the hands of other people, and myself, before I started seeing my world from a higher perspective, through the eyes of Spirit. From this perspective, it is far easier to find peace and happiness and to love and forgive others, as well as oneself.

Each of our life experiences, whether good or bad, becomes a teaching lesson for our Spiritual growth. We may not like what is happening in our lives, and we may desperately wish to change our lives yet feel unable to do so. Whether we are aware of this or not, the process of change is readily available to us, at any time. We are never stuck in any way, always having the ability to be the Creator in our life. Once we learn that we are not victims, but rather active players in the life lessons that we have come to experience, we begin to learn the value of self and of others as well. We all have a purpose for being and we are all champions, just by virtue of our very existence.

We can each achieve greatness with a minimum of effort. That effort begins by allowing Spirit to move through us, and that movement begins by acknowledging that we are not alone. There is something out there greater than all of us. That something is the presence of God, in His or Her many forms, but nonetheless, the common thread that binds us all together; our Creator.

As you begin to ask questions about Spirit in your own life, and allow Spirit to move you, you will find your own path much less complicated and more pleasurable. You will find a greater satisfaction in your day-to-day life as you surrender things that have less meaning and embrace those which have a greater Spiritual meaning. You will begin to accept love and offer it to others, unconditionally. Gone will be the anger and resentments of daily life, replaced by an acceptance of your divine inner purpose and the joy that comes from truly living.

After reading this book, I hope that you will think about how many times you remember Spirit touching your life. Did you listen to suggestions whispered in your ear or did you just ignore them and write them off as a silly idea? Were you warned of imminent danger? Did you experience a loved one reaching out from beyond in some unusual manner that cannot be explained by rational thought or science? Have you had a miracle in your life that defies logic? In what ways has Spirit touched you? How many times have you been compelled to do or say something and not known why? That is Spirit speaking through you. How many times have you suddenly thought to do a good deed for someone else? That is Spirit touching another life through you. I bet when you think of it and are honest with yourself, you will find that Spirit has been right beside you all along, helping, guiding and directing you throughout your life.

For those firmly entrenched in their religious convictions, may I suggest that Spirit transcends all religious belief systems. The souls of our brothers and sisters know only love in its purest form, the love that comes from our Creator. Spirit is not prejudiced, biased nor residing within one singular belief system. Spirit loves unconditionally. Most religions teach us a core principal, which is to love. That message is a fundamental truth and the true message that Spirit wishes to convey to all alike, without prejudice, and without regard to dogmatic belief systems.

Spirit teaches that despite the differences in our points of view and religions, there is a common thread binding us all together, a simple pureness longing to be acknowledged. That part of us is Spiritual in nature and is the essence of who we are, the soul part of ourselves. The soul part of us never dies, but continues to live beyond the earth's realm, long after we are through with our physical bodies.

Our loved ones who have passed before us are indeed very much alive in Spirit, and aware of, and involved in our lives. They wish to communicate the message that there is hope, and a life beyond this earthly plane. They wish to convey to us that the purpose for our existence is to learn how to give and to receive love. There is no singularly more important purpose for our being here on this planet, except to love one another, and to grow spiritually in the process.

It is not just timely that we are experiencing more and more indications of Spirit in our lives. It is not just by chance that Spirit is revealing itself through various forms of the media or through unexplained phenomenon. Even with as tragic a situation as the September eleventh terrorist acts where thousands of people lost their lives, out of that tragedy came stories of sightings of Angels following firemen into ground zero, and stories of true miracles by many people. That day, as an example, had a deliberate purpose where Spirit reached out from beyond our dimension to allow us a brief glimpse into its world. I believe that Spirit chose to reveal itself in this manner for our greater good. The globalization of the media projected that choice to the vast corners of the world, awakening in many the possibility that there was something more beyond what we see in everyday life. Those courageous souls, who partook in the experience of such a tragic loss of life, were our teachers. They loved us so much that they chose to sacrifice their earthly lives in order to teach a greater lesson to all of us, one of Spiritual awareness and unity.

We have the capacity now, as never before, to understand the nature of Spirit and to communicate with it as well. We cannot simply grow through technology, or through our biological DNA. The mind, body and Spirit are one, the composite human being, and we are being asked to grow spiritually, now more than ever before.

As long as we remain stuck in the same processes year after year, our Spiritual growth is slow. As human partners growing together on this earth, it is time that we raise our consciousness to accept others around us, and look past our faults, opinions, race, religion, and belief system. It is time that we open ourselves to a higher Spiritual force, one whose origin is that of another dimension. Our Creator is speaking to us directly, and it is time that we begin to listen.

Through opened minds and hearts, Spirit can move through each one of us, awakening us to our true life's purpose. There is much more to life than just what we want at the moment, and what we can gain for ourselves. It is not about territorial possession or political rightness. Life is about loving one another and helping one another to be successful in each other's journey. We must reach beyond the materialistic, self-centered type of thinking that has become commonplace in this century. We must surpass the tendency of others to interject negativity into our lives.

We cannot accept the world merely in the state that it is, we must become creators of a better world. We came down to this planet with a specific purpose, and now we are being called to remember that purpose.

Spirit has a tremendous capacity to love each of us and Spirit wants us to be successful on our life journeys. Spirit desires the ability to communicate directly to us, through us and with us. It longs for us to open our hearts and our minds together, in one united voice. Through prayer of any kind, Spirit has the ability to work miracles, on behalf of our Creator. The love of our Creator is unconditional, pure and vast. We are not alone. We are always joined with our Creator, not as separate beings, but individual components of a larger whole. That whole includes our loved ones who have passed on before us, and the dimension of Spirit.

Throughout the book I outline some of the various ways that Spirit has communicated to me and through me during my life. These events are only some small examples of the many ways Spirit speaks directly to us, if we only listen. It is my hope that you will find parallels with some of my personal experiences, and awake to the process of Spirit moving within your own life. Share this book with others you know. Everyone can benefit from the awakening of Spirit within their life and the knowledge that the greatest purpose we have on this planet is to love.

I personally invite you to allow yourself to be moved by Spirit through the stories on the following pages.

-Spirit thanks and blesses you

* * *

You can't kill the Spirit, it's old and strong –
Just like the mountain, it goes on and on

– the author, (at age 19)

BETWEEN TIMES

The room was semi-dark but had an ethereal quality about it. I was in a rectangular building that had white marble steps and great columns supporting the two-story structure. In this great hall, lives were being carefully constructed and planned, in blueprint fashion. I felt this a place of great importance, and a gateway between all physical and Spiritual planes in the universe.

In the center of the large room, was a huge planning table. The structure glowed in the center, as if the tabletop was illuminated from beneath. I could see the tall windows on either side of the great hall, casting a delicate amber glow of light and love upon everything in the room.

On the center of the table was an enormous map constructed of a dark blue material. The map contained all of the possible pathways of all of the different souls who would interact with me over the course of my lifetime.

There were many intersections on various points of the map and at these intersections, new people, good and bad, would be introduced or woven into the various points of my life where I would have to make critical decisions about how I would proceed.

There were many ancient, white-robed, white-haired and very caring individuals standing around this table, intricately planning the entire course of my life. There was much discussion over who I would meet and when, who would present challenges in my life, and who would be my support team. Every aspect of the moments of my lifetime were carefully attended to in a loving but serious fashion. Absolutely every possible outcome of every incident, no matter how small, was analyzed to ensure the completion of the tasks for which I was being prepared.

As I viewed these beings working together in the planning stages of what would soon become my lifetime, I remember walking over to the table and glancing at one point on the map, after which I asked a question. I was allowed to provide a certain amount of input, but the majority of my future interactions were engineered by the older, wiser beings attending to my life plans. The answer to my question was lovingly presented to me and; having satisfied my concerns, I continued on my walk, leaving the intricate details to those better qualified to make the proper decisions for me.

When the plans were finally completed, the map or chart was rolled up and put into a protective tan cylinder that was then added to a large bank of cylinders. There was one cylinder for every representative soul who would be making their journey to this plane. The cylinders contained a complete Spiritual life plan for each incarnating individual to follow. The individual would always retain the freedom of choice, but the charts held all the preplanned possible outcomes of every event that could either help ensure the success of, or the destruction of the soul's life plan.

After the completion of my life plan, I was sent to another place to speak with the elders, powerful beings who oversaw the planning of each lifetime. I remember there were several of these individuals, whom I perceived to be male and female, but having somewhat generic aspects of both. The "males" had long white beards, which served more as an identifier of Spiritual wisdom than as an indication of age or gender.

I listened to much debate among the elders about how successful my mission was going to be in this lifetime. I remember insisting that although the tasks I was being asked to complete were most difficult, the significance of them was what drove me to accept the mission in the first place. I assured them that despite the difficulty level of the journey, that I would spiritually adhere to my purpose on this plane and that somehow, I knew I was certain to succeed. Given a final opportunity to refuse the mission, I remained undaunted by the upcoming challenge and accepted with great seriousness, the tasks that I was soon to face.

The elders warned me that I may not be properly prepared, but they allowed me to proceed with my journey because I wished it. They communicated to me their concern that I was too spiritually immature to be able to fully understand the complexities of the tasks before me. They decided that I could go ahead anyway, and they would offer me support during the critical points in my mission to help ensure my success. Their job was not to refuse a sincere request for an incarnation, but rather to be advisors to the complexities of our life journeys. Every request for an incarnation is allowed for the individual's greater good. Everyone retains the right of free will, even on the spiritual plane, because the foundation of our Creator is unconditional love.

After my visit with the elders, I returned to the great hall and noticed a marble table upon which I lay down. Once comfortable, some light beings attended to my head and feet, assuring me that the journey would be short. They imprinted the knowledge that I was going to a place that would be very heavy, difficult and negative. They communicated that even though I would not consciously remember them, I would be spiritually aware of the family I had in the ethereal dimension and that they would be around to help and guide me from beyond.

I was assigned a guide, another Spiritual entity who had accompanied me in my journey in the ethereal. This helper would remain attached to me from beyond and serve as my teacher, guide and friend. This being, from beyond, would help guide and protect me from taking the wrong pathways in my lifetime. There would be difficulties of communication between us due to my limited ability to tune in to my spiritual helper; and my free will that could either choose to accept the help that was sent, or dismiss it entirely.

The guide's influence from beyond was offered out of love to me and of all of humanity, to ensure the success of my mission. Because all memories of the ethereal would be "erased" once I arrived at my destination, my Spirit guide would serve as my unconscious memory of both my place of origin and for the purposes of remembering what tasks I had come here to achieve. While his or her unconscious input could help influence the success of my journey, the rest of the decisions would be completely up to me.

The guides, while Spiritual helpers, would not be able to interfere with my free will, relying only on subtle pokes and prods, signs, and their limited ability to communicate through the thickly negative and heavy atmosphere of the Earth environment, to achieve our collective goals. These loving individuals, who themselves had been survivors on the Earth plane, are by virtue completely at our mercy as to whether or not we decide to allow their positive influence or if we choose to ignore them and block them out completely. Unflustered by the prospect of being completely ignored, our Spirit guides lovingly serve us nonetheless, and accompany us always on our lifetime journeys.

I waited for what appeared to be only moments in the Spiritual plane, but on the Earth plane, was apparently my nine-month gestation period. I remember slipping consciously in and out of my adult ethereal body, which was about thirty years old, and into the womb of my

Mother, while waiting for the birthing process to begin.

At times I spent quiet time in the relative silence of the womb, and listened to the soothing sound of my mother's heartbeat and the curious muffled outer world sounds that could be heard from within her abdomen. I heard the tones of people's voices, and although I could not understand the language (because I was not yet born), I took comfort in my pending arrival and the importance of my mission.

I remember feeling insecure and afraid at times, and my soul would temporarily retreat back to the ethereal side, for the love and assurance that had become so familiar to me. After several of these temporary "trips" to the earth plane and back to the ethereal, I said my goodbyes to the loving souls around me and prepared for the final entry onto the physical plane that we all come to know as Earth.

I had my share of reservations for the journey, as I knew this was the last time I would see my Spiritual friends and family for a while. I took comfort in the importance of the mission that I was about to accept and went into it willingly, full-steam ahead.

The ethereal life that I was leaving would soon become only a vague misty memory, and the journey that would become my lifetime would soon be under way. I would forget from where I had come, in a state of blissful ignorance, once I entered the Earth plane. This process was designed to ensure that I could more fully focus on my life, without the distractions of the knowledge of the ethereal plane. If I were to come to the Earth plane and begin a journey, in fairness to me, I would be born into it both physically and symbolically naked, a blank slate from which to start my life.

It would be a very long time before I would have the ability to recall either my origins or my mission in life. In fact, there was no guarantee that I would awaken from my amnesia at all. The task of getting my attention would be left up to my Spirit guide and the Spiritual realm to handle.

* * *

Success is to be measured not so much by
the position that one has reached in life
as by the obstacles which he has overcome.

– Booker T. Washington

FAREWELL FRIEND

I remember my younger brother being born when I was thirteen months old. I recall the day that he and my mother arrived home from the hospital. I saw everyone fussing about and paying them a great deal of attention. Feeling jealous, I decided that I was not too happy about my new brother's arrival and all the attention he was receiving. At one point, my grandmother held me and I looked down at my baby brother, as he lay asleep in the playpen. I heard people talking to me, and although I understood part of what they were saying, I was very frustrated at this thing called language, something I could barely understand and on a lesser level because of my age, barely communicate. I distinctly remember thinking that without the knowledge of the language, I had no idea how it was that I would ever communicate that which I wanted to say.

At the same time, I remember having the ability to hear a voice speaking to me, and the knowledge that it was the voice of my Spirit guide. I know back then that I could still see my Spirit guide. Although I don't remember now what he looked like; other than the fact that he was a Native American Indian, I remember that I could speak with him. We would hold lengthy conversations, although when I spoke, it sounded to others like typical baby babble. And yet I was speaking to my Spirit guide in a language that both of us could easily understand. To others, I was merely making random baby noises, or speaking to the air or no one in particular.

I had a conversation with my guide whereby I asked him how it was that I could still speak with him and simultaneously know a few words of the English language. The guide patiently explained to me that although I could speak with him easily now, very soon, as I learned how to more effectively communicate with my Earth parents, my ability to interact with him would be closed off. This was for my greater good I was told, as the Spirit guide's job during the time I was an infant, was to accompany me and make me feel safe and loved until I was able to form an attachment with my Earthly family. Once that connection took place, the Spirit guide's role as a support person would fall into the background, as he would from then on, be forced to influence me in an unconscious manner, so as to not interfere with my life plan.

Although I did not want to terminate the communications with my Spirit guide, I knew that if I still wanted to go forward with my life's mission, that the conscious connection to the ethereal plane would need to be substituted for an unconscious one. This was the point where my Spirit guide asked me if I still wanted to continue forward in my life, as it was the last opportunity for a while (last rest stop if you will), as I traveled forward on the road that would become my life.

Within the brief time period between learning the language of oral communication while still being connected with the ethereal plane, we make a conscious decision whether we wish to continue on our life path or if we wish to leave the Earth plane and await a better opportunity to live out our Spiritual mission. I think we are given various times in our lives where we can in effect, duck out the back door and leave this plane, with no questions asked. This first point in my life was a key place where I made the conscious decision to move forward with my life plan.

I want to point out my belief that fetuses, infants and very young children who come to Earth and then leave abruptly thereafter, are simply making their stay as short as possible, for their own reasons, which although unbeknownst to us, are decisions made for our, and their, greater good.

As painful as it may sound, perhaps their original mission was purposely one of a short duration, designed for the Spiritual growth of their family members. Perhaps they just wanted a taste of what Earth life was like before making the decision that their mission was too difficult or that the timing was just not right for them. Perhaps there are other reasons that we as humans, can only attempt to comprehend. Everything truly happens for a reason, and sometimes the reason is not for the purposes that we think. If we can emotionally remove ourselves from a situation, we find that among tragedy or difficulty, there is always a greater Spiritual lesson for all that is to be learned.

We as parents, make the mistake of believing that the children that we bear, adopt, or raise are our property, just because their outward shell takes form from the collective contributions of two physical parental bodies. We forget that we are all children of our Creator, and that we all belong to the family of God, instead of to one another.

We are not property to be held and released, as we think of our children as our children, or our spouse as our spouse. We truly are all independent individuals who are spiritually connected and who each have an important reason why we decided to come down to Earth in the first place. We enter into and leave one another's lives in a constant state of change, always teaching each other and growing through personal interactions and experiences together, in both negative and positive ways.

We forget or perhaps don't realize that the very essence of what makes us human beings is the invisible soul residing within each one of us. Anyone who has had the misfortune of being in the presence of someone who has just died knows firsthand the remarkable difference between a lifeless shell of a soul-less body, compared to that of a soul-filled body in a living, breathing human being.

We ask ourselves why our son or daughter, parent, or loved one, died and left us behind. In reality it is we who have left our loved ones behind when we first came down to this Earth plane from the Spiritual or ethereal plane. In death, our loved ones have simply returned "home" while we remain down here on the Earth, continuing on our Spiritual journey.

Naturally we grieve because we miss our loved ones. If we can eventually put their deaths into a perspective that is instead, appreciative of the soul who has already completed their journey, we can begin to heal and learn important Spiritual lessons. One such lesson is a greater appreciation of the gift of our life here on this Earth.

The passage of time does help to heal all wounds, if we allow the healing to take place and learn from our experiences. We must take comfort in the fact that we will see our loved ones again when it is our turn to move away from the Earth plane, when we have completed our own journey. Know that our loved ones are watching from beyond, and aiding us on our paths.

* * *

Our scientific power has outrun our spiritual power.
We have guided missiles and misguided men.

– Martin Luther King, Jr.

VISITORS

As a child, I spent many years in private emotional turmoil brought about by something that I could not control – child abuse at the hands of one of my parents. At night, one might think that I would experience a temporary reprieve from the day's events. Most nights however, I spent lying on my side curled up in a ball. In my bed I would hide with the covers drawn up over my head.

I lived in fear both in the day time, and at night. I know now that the covers would not have prevented anything from happening to me, but as a child, my bed was my refuge, my savior, and my shield. I prayed every night for relief from what I was experiencing, and yet each new day brought more of the same negativity into my life.

On several occasions, I would be sleeping or nearly so, and I would "feel" the presence of someone in my room. The invisible "someones" would be at the foot of my bed, like a guardian, or a friend, but I could not see them. I probably should have felt frightened by their presence, but for some reason I was always more curious than anything else. When I sensed the guardian to be present, I would feel protected and able to fall asleep.

Some nights I would go to bed, and when the lights were out, I would experience a phenomenon that could only be explained as watching the air around me physically moving. Patterns and textures would suddenly appear in the dark air of my bedroom, and my bed would be enveloped by what would appear to be a moving, living curtain of transparent matter. The shapes and textures would undulate in a manner that appeared to be very much alive. When this would happen, fear would eventually override my curiosity. While I would initially experience curiosity and observe the veil's movements; after a time, the necessity to jump out of bed and turn on the lights and face the reality of what I was experiencing would eventually overcome it.

Some evenings I could hear the muted whispers of people I could feel but not see, through the "veil" that appeared to hang as a curtain around my bed. It seemed as if I was trapped in a world by myself, an island among this dimension that I was allowed to experience, for whatever purpose, on these occasions.

For many years I did not understand what this veil was, to whom the voices belonged, or why I was singled out from many people in this world. I wondered if what I was experiencing could possibly be real. Perhaps I imagined it, I would say to myself, attempting to comprehend what I saw. Maybe it was something that happened to bad children or to kids who were beaten.

Despite my attempts at logical rationalization, I was fully aware that I was awake every time I had one of the experiences, and talked to no one about them, for fear of ridicule.

Despite these glimpses into the "other dimension", my childhood continued to be riddled with verbal, physical, and even a few instances of sexual abuse. When I was seventeen, I finally escaped by being thrown out of the house, but I never forgot the guardian or the experiences that seemed to want to present themselves to me, perhaps out of comfort or sympathy.

Maybe there was a greater purpose for me in life, and the fact that Spirit revealed itself to me would be something that I could share with others much later in life, once I reached a better understanding of it.

* * *

Death is no more than passing
from one room into another.

– Helen Keller

PAPA GOES HOME

When I was about three years old, I went with my family to visit my paternal grandfather, who was ill in the hospital. To the best of my recollection, he had recently suffered a heart attack. Since he was recovering nicely at this point, he was soon to be released.

After watching the familiar gray-haired gentleman I knew as my grandfather sitting in his deep maroon-colored smoking jacket, I remember feeling an odd sensation that I was looking at someone who was not long for this world. I did not know how I knew that fact, but I do remember the feeling that something was going to be happening to him, and soon. For some reason, I felt a strong need to communicate what I was experiencing to my parents. I waited for the right opportunity, as the adults were lost in conversation and no one paid any attention to this tiny little toddler.

Puzzled by my overwhelming feelings, I waited as long as I possibly could, but my concerned little self finally decided to barge in on the adult conversation that had now carried over into the hospital elevator, as we were preparing to leave. "Papa is not coming back," I would blurt out to the stunned adults on the elevator. "No honey, Papa's doing just fine. He'll be home in no time at all, the doctor said so," I remember my mother sternly trying to persuade me. "No, he's not coming back," I insisted, shaking my head and momentarily glancing down at my patent leather shoes, certain of the information I was relaying, and certain that my parents were going to be angry with me for speaking it.

Immediately following my comment, my father cast a harsh look at me foretelling parental annoyance. Perhaps it was my comment that caught him off guard, but his face warned me that I had better drop my insistence at once. No one spoke any more about my observations and we went home, the elevator's occupants now uncomfortably silent.

Just as I had stated, only a few days later my accurate prediction would come true. Papa was gone, succumbing to a second heart attack while still in the hospital. I had somehow foretold my own grandfather's death at the tender age of three, and looking back now, even I feel surprise at the accuracy of my early predictions.

At three, I could not possibly have known the impact that my "abilities" would have on the future of my life. I had no way of knowing that the information that I had shared in the hospital might have come from my Spirit guide or from some other outside source. I did not know that I had been an instrument through which a loving message would be given to my parents to prepare them for my grandfather's upcoming death. I also had no sense that anything unusual might be happening to me at all; I was just relaying information as it came to me.

I am certain that the hospital incident left my parents scratching their heads, perhaps thinking something was wrong with me; that I had some mental deformity. This was the early sixties, and not a time when others readily accepted Spiritual communication. Being so young and innocent, I also had no way of knowing how this ability to communicate with the unseen influences around me would sustain me throughout some of the more challenging moments of my life.

Another interesting aspect of Papa's death was that I felt his presence all around my grandmother's house. As small children, my three brothers and I would spend some weekends overnight at my grandmother's home. It was there that I would have the unmistakably uneasy feeling of a Spiritual presence.

I would feel Papa in the living room and be afraid to be in there all alone. I would feel him at the top of the tall unbannistered staircase leading up to the second floor bedrooms. And I would feel him in the study, by the wall of bookshelves that he built himself. I never told anyone what I was feeling, but somehow, I absolutely *knew* that it was Papa that I was sensing, and that he was very much alive and around us in Spirit.

* * *

The Almighty has his own purposes.

– Abraham Lincoln

AERIAL CYCLIST

At the age of eleven, my girlfriends and I would ride our bicycles around town. Often times we would have to ride across a busy, four-lane road, with traffic speeds of over fifty miles an hour. Because I had witnessed the aftermath of an accident involving a child on a bicycle when I was younger, I was keenly aware of the interval needed to safely cross this particular highway. I was very cautious and even possessed an internalized motto, "when in doubt, wait it out." So I find it more than just a little interesting what happened to me that sunny afternoon.

My three friends and I were each crossing the highway one by one on our bicycles, through relatively heavy traffic. I went last and when it was my turn, it seemed I would never cross due to the large volume of cars. I patiently waited and waited, looking for an opportunity to cross. I tried desperately to ignore the egging on of my three friends, who were growing impatient for me to make my move. I felt the pressure that only friends can provide; yet I was hesitant to cross, for obvious safety reasons. As soon as I found an opening in traffic, I estimated the distance and the rate of speed of the oncoming car. If I hurried, I could just make it across, and eliminate the now loud urging of my friends. Probably because of the razzing of my friends, I did not concentrate enough on what I was doing and I unfortunately misjudged the distance.

I pushed the bike with full force, and got about three-quarters of the way across the road. I suddenly realized that in order to get to the other side safely, I was going to have to mount the bike and pedal as quickly as I possibly could. I watched the car and driver barrel forward, oblivious to me. As the vehicle approached, I tried to place my foot upon the pedal only to have it slip accidentally back to the ground, causing me to loose a few steps and precious time, in the process.

I looked at the car's oncoming bumper and knew in that instant that I had no chance of making it across the road. To make matters worse, the sound of my friends' gasps and the sight of their horrified faces confirmed my doubts. I heard the blast of a car horn from the startled driver, who by now had noticed me too late, and said to myself, "No, God, please, I don't want to die." I closed my eyes, awaiting the impact I felt certain was inevitable.

Then I felt time slow down, and in that moment I thought to myself about all the things I wanted to do yet in my lifetime and how sad it was going to be for my family if I died. I felt troubled that my parents would be mad at me for not being more careful crossing the highway. I thought about the driver of the vehicle and how killing me was going to affect them. I knew they would blame themselves for my mistake. I thought of my friends, my brothers and other relatives and how horrible they would feel if I was gone.

In an instant, I felt the swift movement of what felt like wings and strong arms grabbing and lifting both my bicycle and me. I felt a warm blast of air that lifted me up several inches from the pavement and place me lovingly on the edge of the road, out of harm's way.

The whooshing sound and the warm air of the vehicle blew past us in an instant, and then it was over. I stood startled at the curbside, trying to take in the event that had just occurred. My friends, frightened by what they were sure to see, turned very slowly around to face me, and opened their eyes certain they would be forever changed by what may have become of their friend.

Amidst excited cries of "oh my gosh," and "there's no way you made it," I realized it was clear to my friends that there had not been enough time for me to get across. Yet I felt strangely unafraid, almost comforted by the experience. I vaguely remembered what had happened, but did not feel fear during the moments that had just transpired nor did I remember exactly how I came to land on the roadside.

I had the distinct feeling though that I had been deliberately carried across in order to save my life, but by whom, I did not know or see. So when one of my girlfriends asked me how I got across, I just shrugged my shoulders and said simply "I flew" while I silently thanked my Guardian Angel for the efforts that spared me that day.

* * *

Difficulties are meant to rouse, not discourage.
The human spirit is to grow strong by conflict.

– William Ellery Channing

CLOSE CALL

At age fourteen, I was riding my bicycle to the plaza store near my grandmother's apartment, when an elderly woman stopped me and asked if I would help her put her groceries into the back of her parked car.

I regarded the woman for a moment and felt extremely uneasy. She seemed larger than most elderly women, and though she held in her hand a cane, to me she appeared physically quite capable of sprinting. I thought her appearance odd, and it seemed to me to be one more of a man dressed in an elderly woman's costume and wig than it did a "real" elderly woman.

I had never seen a cross-dressing man before in my life, this was 1975, and that kind of thing was rarely seen on television, so I had no idea that it could even be a possibility. Nonetheless, some part of me felt extreme caution at being in the presence of this "woman".

The well-mannered part of my personality presided however, as I cautiously agreed to assist this person, despite my feelings that something felt terribly wrong. When we approached the woman's vehicle, she opened her rear car door and I began to put the groceries on the floor of the rear seat on the driver's side. From my vantage point, it was entirely unnecessary to enter the car for any reason. It had four doors and I could easily place the bags on the floor without stepping inside the vehicle.

Despite this fact, the woman nervously tried to convince me to enter the car by saying "no, no, you need to climb in and put the bags on the other side of the car." This odd statement threw up a red caution flag to me, as I was raised never to talk to strangers, let alone get into a car with one, no matter how old or nice they appeared to be. As I suddenly hesitated, the woman began to sound more nervous, even angry with me. Perhaps it was the insistence in "her" deep voice or my perception of something in its undertone, but I suddenly heard a very strong voice outside of my head say firmly to me, "do not get into the car".

In that instant, I seemed to be trapped in a timeless moment, as if sleepwalking, where I was fully aware of what I was doing, as the moment seemed surreal and dreamlike. In my mind, I saw a picture of the "woman," but in the next moment, I saw in that picture that the woman was really a man dressed like an elderly lady. I also saw a picture of a small hand ax lying in the trunk of a car.

I snapped out my state, and must have appeared startled, as if someone had suddenly slapped me across the face. I dropped the bag of groceries on the spot and ran all the way back to my bicycle and did not stop pedaling until I got to my grandmother's apartment. I told grandma what had happened and she told me that it was good that I had followed my instincts. I do not know if she actually believed my story or not, but it was clear to her that something had frightened me.

A few nights later, a news report appeared on our local television news channel. A man had been arrested in connection to a recent attempted kidnapping of a young girl about my age. I was stunned to discover that he had been dressing in an elderly woman's costume and had been cited as carrying an axe in the trunk of his car. I knew right then and there that on that fateful day, an Angel had saved me with the gift of knowing.

* * *

No one's death comes to pass without making some impression,
and those close to the deceased
inherit part of the liberated soul
and become richer in their humanness.

– *Hermann Broch*

GRANDMA DON'T GO

When I was a junior in high school, my father's mother, my grandmother, suffered a stroke. As she lay in the hospital recovering from it, my older brother suggested that he and I go and visit her. It was several days after her stroke, and the doctors had told our family that she was recovering and could have visitors. I thought sure, why not, and I agreed to go with my brother to visit grandma.

We arrived at the hospital and spent the afternoon with grandma, talking about pleasant things. When it was suddenly time to leave however, I experienced something unusual. Somehow I simply knew that once I left the hospital, that it would be the last time that I saw my grandmother alive. I did not share this information with my brother, because it frightened me. I did not know where the information was coming from. The knowledge felt like it was being relayed to me in some external manner, because I needed to know, in order to be prepared for what would be happening soon.

I don't know how I was aware of the fact that grandma was not long for this world. I looked at her lying so small on the bed, and I could see nothing different about her. Maybe there was something spiritually about her that my soul recognized, but my eyes could not see. Despite the fact that I kept telling myself "don't think like that," the feeling would not go away. I just did not want to believe it at all, my beloved grandma…would soon be gone.

I resisted my brother's scolding of me because I refused to kiss grandma goodbye before we left. I could not bring myself to let her go, even if it was just I who knew it was her last night on this earth. In my youthful understanding, I loved my grandma so much that I thought somehow that if I did not kiss her goodbye, then maybe it would prevent her from leaving us.

As it happened, I simply told her "see you tomorrow" and waved to her, knowing that it was probably the last time I would see her for a very long time. A few hours later that evening, the phone rang. I knew it was the hospital calling even before my mother answered. I did not have to wait for an explanation, the sound of my mother's voice revealed the truth to me. Grandma was indeed, gone, as I had been told earlier in the day.

Of course I cried, but I also felt strangely at peace. I knew somehow that grandma was still around us, perhaps in a place that was far better than here. I knew that she was not suffering, and I knew that we could not see her. For some reason, perhaps out of her love for me, grandma's soul had already prepared me in advance for her imminent departure, and I was grateful for the experience of that very personal gift.

* * *

Life is partly what we make it,
and partly what it is made by the friends whom we choose.

–*Chinese Proverb*

BEST FRIENDS

As I grew up, I had a pet dog, a yellow Labrador retriever that I had named Barney. He was truly my best friend in every way and he accompanied me in everything that I did. Barney was intelligent and loads of fun. I taught him many tricks and he taught me many things about the animal world and its unconditional love.

Because Barney had so much energy, I had to "unwind" him after each play session or he would come bounding into the house, something of which my mother did not approve. To give Barney the indication that play time was over, he and I would walk once around the outside perimeter of our house and I would talk soothingly to him, encouraging him to relax and calm down. By the time we reached the front of the house again, he would be aware that playtime was over and his demeanor would be once again, calm. In a way, I wondered if Barney was instinctively aware of my mother's dislike of his energy level, which he obediently curbed for me whenever we were done playing.

For many years Barney and I were inseparable, and throughout the many years I endured of child abuse, my dog was the one "person" I could turn to who was sympathetic and loving without question. When it came time to leave my home for the outside world, the hardest part for me was leaving my beloved friend behind, as my mother forbid me from taking my dog with me. As life would have it, eventually, Barney grew old and ready to leave this world. He was diagnosed with some sort of cancer, and as he was forced to undergo repeated operations to remove tumors, I found Barney growing weaker and weaker each weekend that I came to visit my parents' house.

During one such visit, I noticed that Barney looked pitifully more like a famous reanimated monster than he did a dog, with his many incisions closed with staples. He also had a physical presence about him that indicated to me that he was nearing exhaustion. Throughout my visits, he appeared so weak that he could barely lift his head off of the floor to greet me. I knew that it would not be much longer before Barney would die, so I tried to spend as much time with him as possible.

Just before I left one afternoon however, Barney uncharacteristically managed to summon enough strength to get up, and painfully limp across the floor over to where I was standing. As I looked into what I thought would be his sad eyes, I saw instead, a youthful Barney, wanting to go outside and play. "Boy, you can't go out like that," I must have said to him. Nevertheless, Barney wagged his tail and put his nose under my hands as he always did to indicate that he wanted me to take him outside to play.

For some reason, I decided to humor him, after all, he knew better than I did how he felt physically. Outside we went on that warm afternoon, and although Barney could do little else but walk slowly, he somehow found the energy to accompany me as I wandered around the yard. After a few minutes I could see that Barney was growing tired and I decided to bring him into the house via the back door, to save him the steps he would have normally taken around the perimeter of the house.

But my friend was planning on taking no short cuts that day. He insisted on walking toward the front of the house, deliberately disobeying my orders to come to the back door. It was almost as if he was trying to show me something or communicate something to me. I decided to follow him and I walked over to where he was standing. "What's going on boy?" I asked him. When I said this, Barney wagged his tail as if to say, "come on, there is something that I want to do with you." We walked more slowly now, around the entire house, all the way around to the back again, and then all the way around again to the front of the house.

By walking me around the house one final time, my beloved friend was telling me that his time was nearing an end. He had communicated to me with a loving persistence, in a manner that he knew I would understand. When I said goodbye to him that evening, I knew it would be the last time we would be together for a very long time.

That evening, ten miles away in my apartment, I was awakened from a sound sleep by the feeling of a presence in my bedroom. I stared into the darkness and I could see the misty shape of something brownish-gold in color, moving slowly toward me in the darkness. As I watched the mist take shape, I rubbed my eyes and wondered if I might still be sleeping, but I realized quickly that I was indeed, very much awake.

The shape formed a transparent, yet tangible likeness of my dog Barney. He wagged his tail and sat down for a moment. I simply stared at him, without speaking a word. He looked well again, and he appeared to be very happy. Then Barney stood up and turned as if to bound happily away, while the mist evaporated before my eyes.

The next morning, before I had even climbed out of bed, my mother called my apartment to inform me that Barney had died the night before. I replied simply, "I know." Barney's Spirit had traveled the distance through the spiritual dimension to my bedroom, to personally say goodbye to me.

* * *

Angels around us, Angels beside us, Angels within us.
Angels are watching over you when times are good or stressed.
Their wings wrap gently around you,
whispering you are loved and blessed.

– An Angel Blessing

WHO'S DRIVING

It was late one night and my boyfriend and I and his young child were returning from a movie at a drive-in theatre. We were all worn out and I was dozing off in the front passenger seat while Hank's two-year-old child Jenny, slept in the back seat behind me. It was 1980 and wearing seat belts had not yet become mandatory by state law, nor was it a typical concern for most people my age.

As we drove a couple miles from Hank's parent's home with whom he lived, I was drifting off to sleep and was almost completely unconscious. Suddenly I heard a voice announce into my right ear, "wake up, I need you to do something right now." I started to wake a little, so the voice continued, this time more loudly. "I need you to get Jenny and put her in your lap–do it now." With that statement, I became completely alert and sat up, saying to Hank, "what did you say?" Hank glanced at me blankly from the driver's seat and replied, "I didn't say anything." Since it was clear from his remark that Hank had no idea what I was talking about, I simply shrugged my shoulders and settled back into my seat, intent on falling back to sleep.

As soon as I closed my eyes again, the voice reappeared, this time louder and more insistent. "I need you to wake up right now and put Jenny on your lap." The voice was so authoritative and loud, as if there was someone sitting right next to me. I knew that to be impossible, since the car door was the only thing on my right. I sat up straight with a start, and awoke, rubbing my eyes. This time I felt extremely impressed that I needed to do something urgently, although I did not have the slightest clue why.

I looked around, and noticed that we were still a few blocks from home. I realized that Jenny would have to be awakened anyway when we arrived home, but this nagging feeling that I needed to act quickly persisted so strongly that I finally gave in to it. I said to Hank, "I don't know why, but I feel like I need to wake Jenny up and put her on my lap."

As irrational as my request had sounded to me, I was surprised that Hank did not think anything of it, but instead replied, "that's fine." With his approval, I awakened the sleeping child from the rear seat, and despite her protestations, put her on my lap in the front seat, and curled my arms protectively around her. We continued down the road to the next stoplight as I waited for whatever event was to happen next.

Once we arrived at the intersection, I felt extremely uneasy, like something terrible was about to happen to us. Every hair on the nape of my neck stood erect in anticipation. The stoplights were not working, and instead there were temporary stop signs placed at every corner of the street's edge. To the front and to the left there was no traffic in site. To the right, was a big hill, which prevented us from seeing any oncoming traffic from that direction. I felt so nervous about the intersection that I said to Hank, "go slowly through this intersection, I have a really bad feeling about this."

After first coming to a complete stop and peering in both directions, Hank started cautiously ahead. I barked at him, "No! more slowly, crawl!" Startled, he braked just in time for me to notice out my side window, that a green car was careening over the hill. It was traveling at a high rate of speed, with no intention of stopping and we were right in its path.

Because we had been traveling so slowly, the car with the drunk driver impacted our car's right front tire, just in front of the passenger compartment where Jenny and I were seated. The car hit with such a powerful force that it slammed us around inside of the car. I remember hitting the car door with my elbow, and my head hitting the dashboard, the rear view mirror and the back of the seat as I became a moving projectile, all the while cradling Jenny in my arms, trying desperately to protect her.

I remember my perception of time changed to that of slow motion as I bounced around inside the car and prayed silently and urgently, "please God, no broken bones, no broken glass." I was terrified of being injured, or having one or all of us killed.

The car spun around once in a circle and came to rest yards away, facing a new direction, at the curbside. When things quieted down, I realized that we were relatively unhurt, although in reality I was dazed from a concussion and was feeling somewhat confused. We climbed out of the car through the driver's door since mine was jammed shut, and I noticed that the other car's occupants were already out of the car and running away from the scene. Once we were outside of the vehicle, I observed the physical state of my car, which shocked me.

The car was totaled to the point that there was no right front engine compartment at all. The entire engine had been moved aside, displaced terribly from the force of the blow. The metal car frame was twisted, the right front wheel completely caved in, the passenger door jammed and dented, and the right rear quarter panel literally flattened. Yet somehow we had all survived the accident and come out of it relatively unscathed. I also happened to notice that there was not one single piece of broken glass present. Not even a taillight or turn signal light had been damaged in the accident. How odd, I thought to myself, but gave thanks to God for answering my prayer.

I realized later on that a voice from Spirit must have saved us that day, by giving me the explicit directions needed for all of us to survive unharmed. After reviewing photos of the extensive damage to the vehicle, I realized what a close call we had experienced. Without the verbal warning I received which caused the deliberate slowing of the vehicle and the relocation of a small child; if the drunk driver's car had instead hit my door or the rear of the vehicle where the child had been sleeping, neither she nor I would probably be alive today.

* * *

Silently one by one,
in the infinite meadows of heaven,
Blossomed the lovely stars,
the forget-me-nots of the Angels.

– *Henry Wadsworth Longfellow*

ANGEL VISITS

During the early nineteen-nineties, my first husband, our children and I had relocated to Wisconsin from the Chicago area, because my husband had accepted a job transfer. We lived in a suburb an hour southwest of Milwaukee and now we found ourselves facing my husband's loss of his barely year-old job. We had no money to speak of, and because he was twenty years older than me, few job prospects for him. I had quit working when we moved in order to raise our two small children. We had no other choice but to pool all of our cash to purchase some desktop publishing equipment so that I could start my own business. Fortunately that business took off successfully and for five years I worked very hard to create something that would support us comfortably.

Because of long standing problems in my marriage however, the business was continually undermined by my husband's jealousy that I was earning much more money than he was. Along with other problems like marital abuse, and exhaustion at raising my children virtually alone, I was also handling my mother's failing health and her recent interstate move to live across the street from us so I could help take care of her.

Eventually the weight of all the responsibility took a toll on my physical health. Unwisely for me, I decided to get a flu shot from the local grocery store. Bad decision on my part, for fifteen minutes after receiving the shot, my immune system went into overdrive and for the next ten months of my life, I spent the majority of my time in bed, too sick to do much of anything at all.

My business suffered and I had to hire people to do my job work for me as I attempted to gain back my poor health. During this time we were having tremendous marital problems, augmented in part, by my husband being forced to shoulder much of my responsibilities taking care of our two very young children.

I spent some of my time in bed reading books; at least I could still do that, and operated my business from the telephone near my bedside as best as I could. Slowly but surely my health improved enough so that I could function, although my marriage did not. It had been, by that time, ten long years of living with someone who was uninterested in being married and who had a great dislike of giving to anyone other than himself. Add to that mix the fact that I endured physical and mental abuse at the hands of my spouse and I had just about physically and emotionally had it in the marriage department.

One night after reading Sophie Burnham's book, *A book of Angels[1]*, I decided that I would open myself up spiritually to the possibility of Angelic presences in my life. I could use a little spiritual support, since I certainly wasn't receiving much of it from my husband. I longed for a marriage that would work, could work; but I also knew that because of my husband's and my twenty-year age difference, that we were two people from two different worlds and his world did not, and probably would never, include me.

I went to bed one evening, greatly disturbed about the progress of my marriage and the path that it had taken. My husband had refused counseling and I had gone myself despite his protestations. My friends were advising me to divorce him although my religious upbringing and mother protested loudly against that idea.

Not knowing what to do, I prayed to God as I usually did, but I also asked my Guardian Angel to show him or herself to me, so that I could see if I really had one. I felt I needed to know if I was surrounded, protected and being assisted through the difficult times I was experiencing.

While I struggled to fall asleep, I was put off by the loud rumbling of my husband's snoring on the other side of the bed. So I lay sleeplessly in the dark, desperately trying to tune out the noise he was making.

Sometime in the middle of the night, I awoke with a feeling that someone was watching me. As my eyes opened, I saw a brilliant white light about two feet wide, hovering directly above my face. It was way too close for my personal comfort and its appearance absolutely frightened me. I knew somehow that its intentions were not to harm me, for inside the white light I saw a beautiful face of a smiling Angel girl. But my fear could not easily appreciate her appearance as I leaped out of bed in search of the light switch. In my panic, I found myself reacting just as I had done years before as a child, afraid of the sights I experienced then. I remember being admonished by my husband who was annoyed that I had turned on the light and awakened him, and though still afraid, I dutifully turned off the light and returned to bed. I pulled the covers up to my neck and decided right then and there that I did not need to see Angels if they were going to be hovering above my head while I was sleeping. I implored them to please leave me alone for the rest of the night, and they did.

The very next evening I went to bed a little wary at what might decide to reveal itself to me as I slept. I made an effort to declare unconditionally that I did not want any Angels to visit me in the same manner as they had, the night before.

As Spirit usually does, it listens directly and carefully to the words that we choose to use when we communicate with it. Spirit is remarkably pure and obedient. If we say we do not want to see things, we will not see them. If we say we want to see things, we will see them. Be careful what you ask for, because you will get exactly that. Always ask for Spirit to reveal itself in a positive manner in the way that will not frighten or harm you, and in a manner that is best for your Spiritual growth. Also put the white light of the Holy Spirit always around you. Imagine a white light that glows around you as a bubble of light. Within this light place yourself, your loved ones, your house, anything or anyone that you wish to be protected. The white light of the Holy Spirit is loving, protective, and always available.

That night, Spirit listened carefully to my instructions and complied. Instead of hovering directly overhead, Spirit decided that it would instead reveal something different. As I awoke this time to the realization that there was a benign presence in my bedroom, I saw through the darkness, the distinct outline of someone. It was a young man, about my age, and he was merely sitting on the edge of the bed. He was doing nothing at all, just sitting, and strangely I felt not the least bit frightened by him.

I did not think to ask any questions, and yet I knew somehow that this "person" or entity would not harm me. I was imprinted with the idea that I was being shown something that would happen some time in my future. I had no idea who this person was and yet I knew that some day this person would be an important part of my life.

Suffice it to say that I was very explicit with my Spiritual requests after that experience. I decided to inform Spirit in no uncertain terms that I was not yet ready to receive its blessings or nightly visits, regardless of the form or purpose. I closed my mind to the process of allowing Spirit to move through me in this manner, so the nightly visits completely halted once again.

It would take many years before I would be able to identify who the man was that had been sitting on the edge of my bed. As it turns out, the figure represented the man who I would agree to make my second husband. The gift that Spirit revealed to me on that night was a person who, unbeknownst to me, would stand beside me during some of the most difficult moments of my life in the years to come. By giving me a glimpse into my future, Spirit lovingly tried to communicate proof of its approval that my miserable first marriage would soon be ending.

* * *

Your vision will become clear
only when you can look into your own heart.
Who looks outside, dreams; who looks inside, awakens.

– Carl Jung

SAFE ASSURANCE

In 1991 during the first Gulf War, my youngest brother was called back into active duty after serving four earlier years in the U.S. Army. He was stationed in Germany and was scheduled to leave for Iraq in a few months. Because of his experience, my brother the tank driver, was well-rehearsed in military weaponry. Because Martin was going to be one of the first involved in the ground war in Iraq, my father, an ex-military man himself, was understandably concerned for my brother's safety.

My father had the classic type-A personality and had spent his entire adult life working hard to provide for his family of four children. He took great pride in all of our accomplishments. Despite the knowledge that his youngest son stood a good chance of being injured or killed in battle, he tried hard to be supportive of all of us, especially Martin.

Around the clock, my father busied the television with the news channels, studying the Gulf war's progress. As the weeks turned into months, my father became a nervous wreck. Any day now Martin would leave for Iraq, and Dad did not want to hear the news that his son would not be returning home.

On weekends I typically spent a few hours visiting my parents. I was now a married woman with one small child, and another one on the way. During my visit this particular evening, I recognized the intense concern etched into my father's face on behalf of my brother. As the evening progressed, my father seemed unable to tear himself away from the television set.

"Dad, we're going to be going now," I told him, resigned to his self-distraction and because my toddler daughter was hungry and becoming unruly. Just then he suddenly turned toward me and said, "No, why don't you stay and we'll have dinner together?" This invitation was unusual from my father, and more so because only moments before he had seemed immobilized by the media reports. "I think Hannah really needs to go home, she is getting so tired dad, I would love to, really I would," I said over the loud protests of my daughter.

"Please," dad said, and the look on his face told me that he would truly appreciate our company. "All right," I relented, sighing, and decided to stay to dinner for his sake. Something about the way that my father spoke told me that I had better take this opportunity, although I would have liked to be selfish and left. I chose instead, to stay partly because of an odd feeling I had and partly because my father rarely, if ever, asked me for anything.

Dad's favorite meal of all time was Kentucky Fried Chicken. So off he ran to purchase a bucket of bliss, while I spent my time trying to get my now agitated daughter to chill out. I was six months pregnant and I was feeling the pervasive fatigue that comes along with carrying a child. I dismissed my own discomfort as I silently acknowledged how important it seemed to my father that I stay and have dinner with him.

Soon dad returned from his trip and we all sat down to eat our meal. While we enjoyed the food, my mother momentarily walked out of the room. I took advantage of her absence to have a private chat with my father. "Dad," I began. "The doctor told me from the ultrasound I had today, that the baby is going to be a boy." "Hey, that's great news," he said to me, revealing a smile and twinkle in his eye. He had three boys of his own and now he was going to have a new grandson. "But don't tell mom, okay?" I found myself saying. I don't know why it was important to me that we share this little secret. Perhaps it was because my mother and I were never on good terms. For whatever reason, at the time, I just wanted to have something between my father and myself that was ours alone to share.

After dinner was finished and my daughter could no longer endure our visit, I finally conceded that it was time for us to leave. "Got to go dad," I said as I packed up my daughter and brought her things outside to the car. After loading the car with the associated baby gear and strapping my child into the back car seat, I returned to the front porch, where my father was patiently waiting to wave goodbye to us. All of a sudden, I could see the extreme worry return to his eyes, which I recognized to be for my brother Martin. As I reached out to hug my father, to my surprise, I found myself suddenly and quite purposely uttering words into his ear. With extreme conviction and assurance, I heard myself say to him, "Martin's going to be okay." I had no way of knowing that I was going to say those words, and yet I did just that.

The way the words leapt out of my mouth had caught me completely off guard. I felt as if someone else was suddenly speaking through me. As my father pulled away from my hug, his odd expression informed me that I had somehow read his mind. I saw the words "how did you know what I was thinking," within his puzzled facial expression. A grateful but awkward smile began to slowly creep upon his face. Apparently the words I had spoken told him exactly what his soul had needed to hear. And yet we were both curious at my sudden insight; for we had not been discussing what had been weighing so heavily upon his mind.

Spirit had spoken a divine truth to my father that day, and that was the last time I ever saw him alive. A few days later, he died of a heart attack, no doubt contributed to by his stress-filled concern over my brother. Thankfully I had been allowed one last meal with my father before his departure. If I had not allowed myself to accept that opportunity, I would have grieved over the loss of it. Nevertheless, Spirit keeps its promise to all. Martin was released from the army immediately upon the death of my father, and because he had already served so long, given a permanent leave to help my mother financially.

So as father, fate or the Spirit world would have it, even if dad had to sacrifice his earthly life to ensure that his son would remain safe, that was okay with him. As Spirit had said that day to my father through me, Martin would be okay. My son was delivered three months later, the birth of which I am certain, was blessed by the attendance of my father in Spirit.

* * *

The golden moments in the stream of life rush past us,
and we see nothing but sand;
the Angels come to visit us,
and we only know them when they are gone.

– *George Eliot*

MAN IN WHITE

I was working in a less than desirable neighborhood in the city of Chicago, where I had to tolerate the urine-drenched elevator to the second floor, the only way to get to our office at night since the front entry was kept securely locked. Employees needed one key for access to the parking garage, another key to enter the building's front lobby and another key for elevator access to the office. Whenever an employee neglected to lock the front lobby doors, especially on extremely cold winter nights, we would invariably find a street person asleep on the dirty terrazzo floor, blocking the path to the elevator.

At this point in my life, I had seen enough of the poorest members of society to feel compassion for them, and often times I would touch them or talk to them, to see if there was any way that I could offer my assistance. Their usual reply was a request for money, and when I had any to spare, I would offer a dollar or two or ten from my purse and direct them to the mission around the corner for a warm meal.

There were many desperately cold winter nights when I would leave work at three in the morning only to discover a homeless man curled in the fetal position on the frigid concrete sidewalk, a few feet from my building. Although some people cast nary a glance at the homeless, I simply could not ignore the plight of these lost souls.

I wondered how a civilized society could allow these cast offs to suffer as cruelly as what I was witnessing. I always felt that I had to do something, anything, to help them. I mentally toyed with the idea of bringing home a "bum" or two and helping get them back on their feet, but thankfully, logic and personal safety prevailed and I realized I could not single-handedly save the world.

Some nights all I had to give was a blanket from the back of my station wagon. Other nights I had nothing at all but a few dollars or words of encouragement and hope, which I felt did little for these people. I wished that there had been more that I could have done for them, but I was only twenty-three, and I had not yet learned how powerful one person could actually be.

I would like to think that the little efforts on my part that I had extended to these desperate people had amounted to something. Perhaps it would return to me in the form of much needed protection I received early one morning after leaving work. It was three a.m. on a summer morning, and the air was muggy and thick with the smell of the urban smog. On most mornings the employees would leave simultaneously, and check to ensure that each safely climbed into their respective vehicles before heading for home.

This morning as happened occasionally, there was no one else available to leave with me, and I had to exit the building alone. As always, I cautiously peered out the lobby door before unlocking it, and walked outside. The sidewalk was very well lit, and I could see both sides of the entire block. I checked for anyone loitering around the abandoned building across the street from where I worked before locking the lobby doors.

The neighborhood was so quiet that even the homeless people were nowhere to be found. "It's safe," I said to myself, seeing not a soul on the sidewalk. I had been carrying a can of pepper spray on my belt for a month or so now, to hopefully give myself some added protection, in case I would ever need it. I was barely a hundred pounds dripping wet, and a young, short, slightly built woman like myself would probably not stand much chance in the wee hours of the morning from a would-be attacker.

I cautiously walked the twenty feet to the garage door and unlocked the small access panel so I could enter inside and raise the electric door. The garage was huge, dark and scary, and I remember feeling rather uneasy that morning, though I could not physically see anything that would warrant such a reaction from me.

Inside the garage, I unlocked the electric locks of my station wagon, backed the car up to the inside of the garage door, got out of the vehicle and pressed the electric door opener. I reentered the car and when the garage door was fully lifted, backed my car out onto the driveway of the building.

Once the car was clear of the garage door, I checked once more for signs of human life. When I felt safe to do so, I quickly exited my vehicle, taking my keys, and ran inside the garage door to activate the closure button of the electric door. As a shortcut, if I moved quickly, I knew I could push the button and dart under the closing door without having to use and relock the side access door a second time.

For a few short moments, I was vulnerable outside of my vehicle, which was when I first saw him. Darting across the street, walking on a forty-five degree angle toward my vehicle in a hurried, purposeful manner, strode a very tall, determined man, who appeared to weigh about two hundred pounds. I noticed he was wearing a long black leather trench coat, something I felt absolutely inappropriate for the time of year. I also noticed what seemed to be a crow bar in his black-gloved hands. My intuition immediately sensed that he was definitely not out to meet me, and startled, I warily observed the man who was now less than fifty feet away from me and approaching quickly.

Mentally I tried to estimate the amount of time it would take me to enter my vehicle, start the engine and pull out of the driveway to safety. With a crow bar in his hand, I reasoned that I would not stand a chance if for some reason my car failed to start or if I fumbled with the keys or whatever else might possibly happen. I knew that a window could easily be broken with a tool like that, and I knew in that moment that I had perhaps seconds before my life was absolutely in danger.

Desperate to escape but at the same time knowing that my fate was nearly sealed, with my right hand I attempted to open the driver side door. Sadly I realized that on my way out of the vehicle I had accidentally activated the electric door lock and I could now not get in without a key. With both hands I hurriedly found a key on the key ring and placed it into the car door lock but in that swirling moment of fear, I had wrongly selected my all-too familiar apartment door key instead of the driver's door key.

With an impending sense of doom, I suddenly remembered the can of pepper spray located on the belt loop over my left hip. With my left hand, I unsnapped the holster and grabbed the can and turned to face my would-be attacker, who was now at the rear end of the station wagon. I was clearly out of time and now I was going to have to defend myself. In that instant, I desperately prayed for someone, anyone, to exit my building and help me face my attacker and perhaps rescue me.

Unfortunately for me, there was no one else around and I was completely alone with a man that I felt was planning to rob, rape or perhaps even kill me. I knew that I absolutely did not want to die, but I felt inadequately able to defend myself. I started praying while I clutched the can of mace, my only lifeline, tightly in my hand.

All of a sudden without warning, the strangest image flashed in the corner of my eye. I "saw" a tall man, about the same size as my attacker, dressed in a white suit with white pants and white shoes, exiting my building's front door. I had never seen this individual before, and I knew there was no reason someone would be dressed all in white in this part of town. The thought of a man dressed in white was odd to say the least, but I didn't care how he was dressed, just that someone was actually going to come to my rescue. The would-be attacker turned his face toward the front door of the building to look at the man, and immediately stopped in his tracks, and turned around. It was as if he knew beyond a doubt that he was about to be caught and then aborted his attack at the very last possible moment.

Instead of attacking me, the man ran quickly across the street and disappeared into a nearby gas station. I stared breathlessly in the attacker's direction, feeling the intense pounding of my heart in my chest. Once I caught my bearing, the thought "what just happened," came into my head. Stunned at the turn of events, I turned to the front of the building to thank the stranger who had just saved my life. Oddly there was no one in the doorway, or on the sidewalk for that matter. It was then that I noticed that the lobby doors were quite visibly closed.

Where was the man in white, and where could he have gone, I thought to myself, bewildered. Forgetting all about safety, I ran over to the front door of the building and noticed that it was still very much locked, and yet I had absolutely seen the man exit the building with my own eyes. My terrified, adrenaline-pumped mind raced. How did I escape being a victim? Who was the man in white and where did he go? Did I somehow just experience an Angelic rescue? Why don't you tell me?

* * *

For He will command His Angels concerning you
to guard you in all your ways.

– Psalms 91:11

DIVINE DONUTS

I was twenty-four and living on a top floor of a three-story walkup apartment in a changing neighborhood of Chicago's Rogers park in the early '80's. I was recently blessed with new neighbors who lived below me, and who also liked to party all night and well into the next morning. Since I suffered from frequent migraines, when my headaches and the party atmosphere below clashed, I had a hard time sleeping. It was awful and many times I went to work completely exhausted. I did my best not to complain, due to my awareness that I was a single woman living alone, and did not need any type of adversity at that time of my life.

One night I could not take any more of the typical into-the-wee-hours partying that occurred in the apartment below mine, so I reluctantly called the apartment manager, who lived on the first floor in another wing of the building. I asked him to please find a nice way to ask my neighbors to turn down the music as I had a headache and had to go to work the next day. I urged him to do it as nicely as possible, and also to please be certain not to tell them who had called. He assured me he would do as I requested, and soon I heard the music turn down amidst some protests at the party, so I drifted off to sleep.

The next morning as I lay in my bed, barely awake, I heard someone say to me, "Get out of bed and go to the store and buy some chocolate covered donuts." I awoke groggily and said unashamedly to no one in particular, "I don't want chocolate donuts; I don't even like chocolate donuts."

I rolled over and put the pillow on my head, wanting to go back to sleep. I continued to hear "the voice," which was persistent, and which patiently repeated itself, this time more firmly. "Get out of bed and go to the store and buy some chocolate donuts. You like chocolate donuts." I took the pillow off my head and said to the air, "I don't want any chocolate donuts." But the voice again insisted, "You need to go to the store and buy some donuts."

The strange command was soon joined with a sudden and painful feeling in the pit of my stomach. "Oh good grief," I said again, to the voice and the air, *"Fine* can I at least take a shower first?" I said half-joking, partly annoyed at the invisible voice that had been speaking. I did not feel weird about the voice, since I had just been sleeping, and since in other times of my life, I had heard warnings and things like that from a similar source.

Once fully awake, I thought I imagined the conversation and that perhaps my stomach was just trying to communicate its state of hunger. Yielding to its wishes, I started for the bathroom, not wanting to have the folks at the grocery store see me looking like I had just crawled out of bed.

Just then the voice got very loud and demanded sharply, "Now! Leave now!" "Okay I'm going!" I said with extreme annoyance, and I continued speaking under my breath as if my parents had sent me out the door on an errand I did not want to do.

All the way to the store, I was wondering why on earth I wanted these donuts so badly. I got to the store, picked up the first box I saw, and was forced to stand in line for almost ten minutes. Apparently there were lots of people that morning that had made the decision to shop. For some inexplicable reason, there was only one inept cashier working the register and it was taking much longer than was really necessary, which I found extremely frustrating.

When I finally did return home with my food, I walked up the three flights of stairs and went to insert my key, but found the front door slightly ajar. I heard the excited chirping of my caged birds, as if in response to someone walking around the apartment.

As I realized what was happening, I dropped my food and ran back down the stairs to call for help. After banging on several apartment doors and receiving no answer whatsoever from any of them, I eventually made my way outside to a gas station, to call for help. I kept watch from my safe vantage point, but saw no one leaving the apartment building; at least not from the front lobby.

It seems that out of forty-four units, only my apartment and the manager's apartment had been robbed that day. When the police opened up the apartment, they found no assailants, but they did find a large butcher knife left conspicuously on the couch. I would presume its planned use would have been to slice something open, but more than likely it was not chocolate donuts, if you know what I mean.

After the crime scenes were cleaned up and all was quiet, I sat by myself surveying the damage to my things. I felt violated and afraid and wondered how long it would take for the maintenance crew to repair the damage to my front door, which was barely hanging by its now bent hinges.

As I looked around the apartment, I probably correctly assumed that the robberies had been in retaliation for the previous night's complaint about the noisy party. Shaken but relieved the ordeal was more or less over, I quietly sat at my kitchen table.

After a few moments I casually regarded the box of chocolate covered donuts I had been so forcefully sent to buy, earlier that morning. In a grateful manner, I said a verbal "thank you" to God and my Guardian Angel for looking out for me. At long last, I finally ate my breakfast, which I realized had been heaven-sent.

* * *

But all God's Angels come to us disguised.

– *James Russell Lowell*

THE MESSAGE

Quite by coincidence, or perhaps by Spiritual intervention, I once found myself traveling through a town that I had lived in some years before when I happened to see some good friends standing outside of a funeral home. I felt an overwhelming urge to stop and see who had passed away. It was not just out of curiosity, but rather a weird, compelling feeling that I had an important job to do.

For whatever reason, I pulled into the parking lot, and stepped out of the car. I am sure that I drew some disapproving glances from some of the attendees, because dressed in a T-shirt and jeans; I was far from properly dressed for the occasion. After meeting with my friends, I was dismayed to discover that an old neighbor of mine named Robert, had recently died. I had attended this neighbor's open house and spoken with both he and his wife Phyllis on many occasions, and considered them friends. Despite my inappropriate attire, I felt the strong need to go inside for the visitation.

As I chatted with Robert's widow, I apologized for the way that I was dressed and gave her my sincere condolences. Strangely, as I looked at my neighbor's body, I sensed that he was somehow standing right behind me, as if to witness his own wake. I did not feel the typical sadness that I felt at other wakes. On that afternoon, I felt a sense of peace instead.

Afterward I drove myself home, which was over an hour away and by the time I reached my living room couch, I noticed that I felt extremely tired. I took an impromptu nap on the sofa and fell immediately into a deep slumber.

I do not remember if I dreamed anything else or not, but just before awakening, I suddenly experienced a strange visit that seemed more like a message, a reaching out if you will, of someone to me. In the dream, I saw a dark faceless shadowy figure and I asked the figure who "he" was. I could sense that the being was male, and I heard him say, "I am a father." I did not understand what he was telling me so I asked him for clarification. "Are you my father?" I asked, since my own father was deceased. "No," was all he replied.

Then the spirit walked or glided rather, toward me and I saw myself from the perspective of the couch in my living room. As he approached me, he reached out his black robed arm or hand, but all I saw was black. Then I felt the distinct, strong touch of a man placing his hand firmly upon my shoulder, which startled me so much that I awoke. We all know what it feels like to have someone put his or her hand on us when we are sleeping–it is very startling. This dark shadow of a man put his hand on my shoulder and his touch was so powerful that I could still feel its presence well after I was awake.

Once alert, I knew that the visit from the Spirit had been no accident. I had a mission. I had been reading a book by the talented medium, James Van Praagh, titled *Talking to Heaven.*[2] The book discussed the afterlife and the idea that we do not die, but that we live on in Spirit. I remembered my neighbor's widow and how full of sorrow she seemed at the wake. Somehow I suddenly got the idea that I was to take a copy of the book that I had just finished, and send it to the woman.

Instinctively I knew that the shadow man who had reached out and touched me on the shoulder was Robert and he was attempting to use me as a vehicle to communicate a message to his beloved wife. That message was that we do not die, but that our Spirits live on beyond our lifetime here. Suddenly I was given the idea to open the book.

As I flipped through the pages unaware of the reason I was searching through them, I suddenly stopped at the beginning of a chapter. I got out a highlighter marker and underlined two phrases in the book. Though I do not remember the book's page number or the exact words any longer, I do know that the phrases contained a very powerful message meant for one reader to hear.

I packed the book into a box and mailed it immediately off to my neighbor's widow. Only after I completed the task did I feel like I was "off the hook," from my sudden obligation and that I could finally relax. There had been something so powerfully moving that the Spirit world needed to relay and I was being used as an instrument to convey that message.

Some weeks later when I least expected it, I noticed a small card arrive in my mailbox. There was no return address, so I was perplexed at who would send the card. I opened the envelope and read the note.

It said something like this: "Thank you so much for your inspired message. I now feel that Robert is resting beyond and is able to see his family. Without that knowledge I know that the pain of losing him would have been most difficult for all of us to bear. Bless you. Love, Phyllis."

The Spirit of Robert had used me, as a vehicle to communicate this important message to his remaining family. The message was that our loved ones do not merely die, but are alive in a Spiritual form and remain connected with us long after they leave us.

* * *

Around our pillows, golden ladders rise,
And up and down the skies,
With winged sandals shod,
The Angels come and go, the messengers of God!

– R. H. Stoddard

MIDNIGHT HAND

Newly divorced, I had gone through the usual stages of separation, anger, grief, and all the bad stuff. I was wondering how in the world I was ever going to pull my life together again. I was financially destitute, as the divorce had left me with tens of thousands of dollars in bills related to a business that had been forced to close. I left my marriage with nothing, and found myself having to relocate my children and self to a completely new environment, miles and miles away from where we had previously lived, so that I could be near my new place of employment.

My ex-husband of eleven years had been harassing me relentlessly since I had received placement of our two children and I had to endure weekly exposures to verbal abuse, and manipulations of the visitation schedule to suit his own whims.

Added to this was his continual filing of court motions in an attempt to get custody reversed and placement granted him of our children. The stress that the family and myself in particular had endured at his hands was relentless.

Fortunately I had formed some new friendships since the time that I had divorced and they were helping me get through the difficult days one encounters when one is attempting to rebuild a shattered life. My children handled the situations as best as they possibly could, but I was always left alone at night, wondering if I had made the right decision.

I knew that I had been married to a verbally and physically abusive man, and that our situation was not healthy either for myself or for my children. Despite the divorce separating us, I wondered if the continual onslaught of abuse from my ex-husband was ever going to stop. Would he ever just leave us alone and get on with his life?

On one particular evening I went to bed, mulling over the day's events. I prayed as I usually did just before settling down to rest. This evening I felt the weight of my pain as the tears welled up in my eyes. They were tears of heartbreak and uncertainty that threatened to interfere with my desire for sleep.

I did the best that I could to bury my feelings, telling myself that I was strong, that I could survive this and that everything would be okay. But sometimes when we tell ourselves this, it is simply not enough. Tonight even though I knew that we would come out of everything okay, I still had doubts. Alone, I drifted off into troubled slumber and longed for comfort.

Around midnight of the same evening, I remember suddenly awakening from a deep sleep. I did not dare to move, because in the darkness, I felt sure that there was a big, strong person absolutely holding onto my right hand. Someone is holding my hand, I thought to myself, alarmed yet intrigued at the feeling. It was the middle of the night and I was supposed to be by myself and there was someone in my bedroom and they were holding my hand!

As frightening as that sounds, in some way I knew that the person who I could not see holding my hand was doing so out of love, in an effort to comfort me. It is amazing when you open yourself up to the possibility of Spirit how easily Spirit will make its presence known to you.

I did not dare move my hand lest the feeling of peace and comfort that the invisible hand provided me would disappear. And as I looked down at my hand, it was clenched in a position that would appear to be one of grasping another's hand. Yes, there was something tangible yet invisible in my hand. Spirit was making itself known through an invisible hand of support in the middle of the night.

Rather than question the experience, I thanked Spirit for the kind offering and fell back asleep, blissfully aware that God cared about me enough to lend me His loving hand in comfort.

* * *

The Angels light another star
Each time there is a birth
To celebrate each precious child
The good Lord sends to earth.

– An Angel Quote

TINY VISITOR

As long as Lydia could remember, she had wanted to have a child of her own. Her health growing up had been littered with reproductive problems. Despite her difficulties getting pregnant, she and her young husband Mack kept trying.

They visited a gynecologist who had the unfortunate task of telling Lydia that she had uterine fibroid tumors, and little chance of carrying a baby full-term. There simply was not enough room in her uterus for both a baby and the tumors. She was advised to have surgery to remove the growths prior to getting pregnant. If she managed to get pregnant, she was well aware of the fact that she risked losing the child because of her precarious health situation.

Despite the doctor's stern warning, Lydia was driven to try to conceive and after a few months, she and her husband Mack were successful. Putting the concerns about the tumors aside, she dove headfirst into books on pregnancy and happily shopped for clothing for her unborn child.

One weekend while visiting Lydia, I made a comment on the size of her tummy, and placed my hand upon her lower abdomen. I already had two children of my own and it had been a long time since I had felt a pregnant tummy. In touching her abdomen, I was fully expecting to feel the typical kicks and nudges that accompany a growing fetus in the womb.

As soon as I placed my hand on Lydia's tummy however, a wave of something overcame me, and I did not like the feeling at all. In my mind's eye I saw a dark image, a field of black shall we say, that felt like death to me. Alarmed, I quickly pulled my hand off of her abdomen.

"What's wrong?" asked Lydia, her eyebrows raised in surprise. "Oh, uh, nothing, I just felt the baby kick" I responded, in defense of my sudden jerking action. I knew in that moment that something was going to go terribly wrong with her baby. I did not want to be an alarmist or scare Lydia with any comments on my part, lest I hopefully be wrong. I wisely decided to keep my mouth shut, but the incident had me literally spooked. I left without saying another word about what I had felt.

The night before Lydia's baby was born, I awakened from a dream where I was being shown a calendar. "Closer, I can't see the dates" I had said in the dream. I saw a picture of a calendar, now much more close-ly, and I noticed three dates on the calendar. I was being shown the 27th, the 28th, and the 29th of a month. I also saw a big black cloud that start-ed out in my abdomen and then suddenly dropped and fell out of my body. I felt like I was losing a baby in the dream.

When the calendar finally zoomed in more closely, I was shown the twenty-seventh day of the month. The dream was so disturbing to me that as soon as I awoke, I immediately added it to my dream journal, which I kept by my bedside. I was unsure of its significance, but I absolutely knew that something bad was about to happen. I remem-bered my pregnant sister-in-law and thought that later on in the day that I should call her, just in case, to check on her progress. It had been two weeks since I had put my hand on her abdomen and had felt the same type of black cloud that I experienced in my dream.

In her sixth month, Lydia had an ultrasound that had shown her baby was growing too slowly because her fibroid tumors had increased in such a way as to compromise the space in her uterus. She sadly developed complications with her pregnancy that would soon lead to the emergency delivery of her premature baby. Her water broke two months before the baby's due date and also on the twenty-seventh day of the month, the very morning I awoke from my horrible dream.

The delivery, because it was an emergency, demanded that the sur-gical team act quickly. From the information I gathered after the deliv-ery, I discovered that the doctors had cut open Lydia's uterus and found themselves bathed in blood. One of the larger fibroid tumors was locat-ed immediately below the incision site and had been incised during the delivery. One thing led to another and Lydia's tiny infant son was quickly delivered through a mass of tissue and blood.

In the process of the delivery, although the doctors and hospital staff refused to acknowledge who or what caused the injury, a surgical scalpel accidentally slashed the tiny infant's left side. He now had an incision from his armpit to his groin, which also managed to lacerate many of his internal organs, critically wounding him.

The tiny baby was immediately brought into the infant ICU and the doctors and nurses were scrambling just to keep him alive. He was no larger than a doll, weighing just over one pound. Tragically, the damage to his internal organs was so severe that it was obvious to everyone present that the boy was not going to survive his horrific injuries.

He lingered in a coma-like state for four hours as the entire family gathered around his bedside, to offer support to the baby's father, Mack, who was in a state of shock. Upstairs in another part of the hospital, Lydia was sleeping off the anesthesia, totally unaware of the problems with her newborn son.

After my husband and I arrived at the hospital, I took one look at the extent of the baby's injuries and instantly knew that the child was not going to survive much longer. I started to think "I should pray," but the feeling in my heart was that I knew he would be leaving and I felt that praying for his survival was not necessary. Somehow I was made aware that he was not intended to stay. I heard one doctor yell at the nurses in frantic desperation for any medication that might help keep the child alive despite the massive injuries and large blood loss that I watched disappear down the tiny infant's chest tube.

"Go to Lydia and get her nurse to bring her down here," was the voice I heard outside of my head, and to my right. I knew the sound of "the voice" from the many instances in my life where it had helped save me from danger. I knew the gravity of the situation and also sensed the short amount of time that remained. I knew that Lydia would not have a chance to hold her son while he was still alive if we didn't act quickly, and I felt that I absolutely had to do something about it.

"Let's go," I said to my husband. "We have to get Lydia down here, right NOW," I said as I pulled his arm, leading him out of the ICU waiting area. We headed up the two floors into the maternity ward and spoke to the nursing staff on her floor. "But you don't understand," I said to the nurse who indicated that Lydia would be up and around in about four hours. "She doesn't have that kind of time," I urged. I explained to the staff that Lydia's baby was already dying and asked for them to call the ICU to verify my story.

Only because I pressed the issue, the nurses finally called the ICU to obtain the necessary permission to remove Lydia from her bed. Despite the fact that she had not yet recovered from general anesthesia, she would be whisked down to the intensive care unit to visit with her dying infant.

Although it was very hard to pretend that I did not know what was going on when Lydia asked me how her baby boy was doing, I said simply, "Mack will be up in a minute and he's going to talk to you." The expression on my face told Lydia that something was very wrong and she started to cry as Mack entered her room. My husband and I left the room to give them some privacy and moments later the nurse brought a sobbing Lydia out of her room along with her husband Mack.

It was hardly three minutes before we arrived at the baby's table where the life support systems were keeping his tiny body functioning as best as they could. I could see that his vital signs and color had already seriously declined from the time that we had first gone up to get Lydia. I knew that it would not be long now before the baby left this world for good.

The doctor turned to a still groggy Lydia and her husband Mack and the decision to let the baby go was painfully communicated to the doctor, who was also clearly upset. I could see the pain on the faces of everyone attending the dying infant and a chill of recognition for their great empathy and heroic efforts overcame me.

Because of all of the suffering the baby had already endured, and all of the suffering he would likely endure in the days to come if he could survive by heroic measures, the difficult decision to baptize him and take him off of life support was made.

The priest arrived and baptized the baby in the presence of the family, which included about ten of us. I was so honored to be in the presence of this tiny child both as he was being baptized as a child of God and while he was preparing to leave this world.

Only moments after his baptism, the little boy's now comatose body was taken off of life support so he could let go of his grip on the physical plane and return to the Spirit world. His tiny lifetime of only four hours, a mere blink of an eye in the grand scheme of things, would leave behind a wake of tremendous blessings.

Several family members, including myself, took turns holding the deceased infant, and I noticed that each member instinctively rocked the baby in their arms. Although my first reaction was that I was a little reluctant to hold a deceased child in my arms, my feelings were quickly overcome with the importance of sharing my brother and sister-in-law's grief.

Upon reflection, to my surprise, the family members who actually held the baby would turn out to be the ones who had needed the most healing in their own lives. Though tragic and terribly short, the circumstances surrounding the arrival and the departure of this special infant left an indelible impression on a great number of people.

His birth gave the gift of Motherhood, however brief, to a woman who had longed for a baby. He gave healing to a Grandmother who had lost a child, years before through a stillbirth. He provided healing to a family member who had lost a child through an unwanted abortion in a violent past. The baby provided me with a new appreciation for my own children, whose births had also been very difficult. He provided healing to his own father, a man who needed to learn the value of family. Lastly, he provided all of the doctors and nurses involved in his birth and death a great many lessons about which I can only begin to hypothesize.

How powerful are we as Spiritual beings, no matter how small, that we can offer so many lessons and affect so many lives in a positive manner, just by virtue of our being here on this planet, even for the most brief of a time period?

Lydia and Mack would go on to recover from the grief of their infant son's death. Soon Lydia had the necessary surgery to remove the troublesome tumors. Lydia became pregnant for a second time, and this time the baby arrived within a normal gestation period. He was delivered a bit prematurely by cesarean section yet arrived both healthy and happy.

At the birth of the new baby, it was a time of elation and joy because of the hardships Lydia and Mack had endured with the tragic death of their first child. In the hospital, my husband and I and children visited Lydia and the new baby, to welcome him into the family.

Everyone took turns holding the child, but as soon as I picked him up and held him in my arms, I felt a kind of physical, electrical shock that was unlike anything I had ever felt before, and it wasn't static electricity. It was a Spiritual energy that permeated every fiber of my being, like it had taken hold of my soul and shook its hand as if to say, "Hey, I know you, do you remember me?"

In the moment that I received this peculiar wave of energy, the idea flashed in my mind that I was actually holding the very same infant that had passed away just a year before. Yet here he was, returning to the same family in a brand new body, unlike the one in which he had traveled last year. That body, because of the physician's accident, had been unable to physically sustain him and he was required to return to God until another body could be created that would support him in his new life.

I don't know how to describe the feeling except that I absolutely knew, at a conscious and Spiritual level, that the new baby was the very same soul who had visited this family for such a short time, only a year earlier.

The instant recognition I felt upon holding the infant startled me so much that I had to put him back down just a few moments later. I asked his father to take him from me, and nearly called the child by his deceased brother's name, which also surprised me. I was so moved by what I had experienced holding the baby that I excused myself from the room and went into the hall for a breath of air and to clear my head, to try to figure out what I had just experienced.

I cannot explain what happened or how I knew, but I feel certain that within that singular experience, I gained confirmation that reincarnation actually does exist. In my heart, I had recognized the baby's soul energy and realized how connected our loved ones are to us, both in life and in death. I know now that people who lose a loved one not necessarily lose that soul forever, but that sometimes, the vehicle that is the human body is incapable of sustaining life and the soul must leave to await a time whereby it can come forth, in a new body, to continue its journey on the physical plane.

I am in awe at the experiences that I have been privileged to feel firsthand, and know what a tremendous gift the soul of my nephew gave to me through the proof of its existence in not one body, but two. Being raised in a traditional religion, I was never taught about reincarnation and even pooh-poohed its existence until fairly recently when my newly opened mind began to look for answers to life's questions. Now I had physical proof that reincarnation actually existed, of that I was absolutely certain.

* * *

He that loseth wealth, loseth much;
he that loseth friends, loseth more;
but he that loseth his Spirit loseth all.

– Spanish Maxim

INSTANT CHANGE

When I was originally going through my nasty divorce, I remember having an attorney who was not giving me proper legal advice or good representation. I had gotten into the habit of asking my deceased father for answers to major questions I had in my life. I would simply ask him yes or no questions out loud and then look for confirmation in the form of pennies and other signs.

In the past, I had obtained answers from my father on many matters through this common method of ethereal communication. You could put it down to coincidence that I would just "happen" to find coins right after asking questions, but I must say that I find it more than a little peculiar that I don't usually find pennies or other coins, ever, unless I first ask my father a question. I went ahead and asked my dad if he thought I should get rid of my attorney and hire someone else to complete the task. I asked for him to send me pennies as confirmation if I should replace the man.

After asking my question, I suddenly realized that I needed to go to the bank and make a deposit. This was a Saturday and I noticed on the clock that it was nearly noon, which was when the bank would close. I hurried along to get to the bank on time. There were quite a few cars in the drive-through and I knew that I would not make the deposit on time so I decided to head into the bank on foot. I was more than a little pleased that there was only one other person in line ahead of me, and I was relieved at the fact that I would be able to make my deposit timely.

A lady in front of me had come into the bank to drop off some coins, and I could see that she had several plastic bags. When she had finished with her transaction, I came to the counter next and inquired about the coins the previous customer had exchanged. I thought that perhaps the woman might have dropped off coins that would be of interest to my two children, who were avid coin collectors.

"All she left were these pennies," said the teller, holding up one of the bags. Inside the bag were very dirty looking grayish pennies, which I immediately identified to be made of steel. "Can I buy those?" I excitedly asked the teller. "Sure, I don't like dealing with these, they are too dirty for me," she replied, glad to exchange the coins with me. "Thanks a lot!" I said to the girl, and put the bag into my purse to take it home where I could examine my prize more closely.

I arrived at my home and pulled the bag of coins out of my purse, while simultaneously turning on the television set. I put the bag of coins on the coffee table and reached for the remote control. The television set was broadcasting a home shopping channel, and just as I was about to press the remote and switch stations, I realized that the program was advertising coins for sale. They were selling perfectly minted sets of 1943 steel pennies, at a rate of twenty dollars per set of five.

"Oh my gosh!" I declared, suddenly. "Look at that!" I said to my dogs, sitting on the rug nearby. I counted out the number of steel pennies that were in my plastic bag and the number came to forty-three. I thought it more than a little odd that at the very same time as I happened across steel pennies, here they were, on the television set, being sold for much more than what they were worth.

It suddenly dawned on me that my father had answered my question. I started thinking about the sign, which was now very obvious to me. "Steel pennies…steel pennies" I said to myself. "Stealing pennies–I get it!" I exclaimed. I realized that my father was trying to get my attention by telling me that the answer to my question was that the attorney was stealing my pennies–stealing my money, or better yet, not a good investment and that I should replace him immediately.

I did replace the attorney right away, who I later found out had been born in the year 1943–and it was the best decision I made at that point with respect to counsel. I am absolutely certain that on that day, I had truly received pennies from heaven.

* * *

And with regard to asking God for monetary help...

Once I received an instant offer of money soon after I had requested it from God. "Okay God, if you want us to go through with this court appeal process, you're going to have to send us a whole lot more money." I would find myself saying out loud to my Creator one day.

The very next day my second husband received a generous offer from his boss, the owner of the car dealership where he worked. His boss suddenly offered during a conversation, "whatever you need, just let me know. Whether it is money or anything else, you just tell me and I will help you."

The very next day I also received a surprising offer in the mail. It was a notice from my credit card company; the same one who had refused to raise my credit limit just a month prior. The offer said that the company had decided to raise my credit line to $25,000.00, claiming that I deserved it. The credit increase would be more than enough funds available to help us afford the cost of the attorney for the appeal. Here was an instant piece of evidence that Spirit does indeed, listen to our prayers, if we just let go and let Spirit take care of our needs.

* * *

Every man has his own destiny:
the only imperative is to follow it,
to accept it, no matter where it leads him.

– Henry Miller

SPIRIT SIGNS

During the many years that followed my divorce, my ex-husband tried time and again to gain custody of our two children. At one point he filed false allegations of child abuse in a desperate attempt to get our children, because I had remarried. During the long months prior to the trial, I had asked for various signs to be shown that we would be victorious in court.

On a morning where I was again at my wits end, frightened of what I was having to face, I asked God to send me a sign. I specifically asked if He would send me a feather, as a sign to prove that we would ultimately be victorious in court. I was searching for confirmation, and thought that a feather would be something that was a little uncommon. I started looking for a feather all throughout the day, but did not find one. I went to work, a little disillusioned that perhaps I was not going to get my sign.

Around two-thirty in the afternoon, my co-worker suddenly got the idea of cleaning out a workroom storage closet. I saw her walking by my desk carrying a cardboard box. I just happened to glance in her direction, probably because she did not normally carry large boxes around the office. Nevertheless, her movement caught my eye and I looked up in time to notice a large corporate logo emblazoned on the side of the cardboard box she carried. It was a feather and there was my sign. Because I am human and a bit stubborn headed, I still did not fully believe we would win. Again, I was seeking confirmation by means of a sign of some sort.

I have since learned that for some reason, when I ask for a sign, it usually happens to reveal itself at the same time of day for me. I don't know if the souls in the hereafter are not morning people or what the story is, but when I ask for a sign, it always appears to me late in the day.

This day was just like previous days, and I was very worried about the trial hearings and the final outcome. (The process lingered for several years, a very long time where I asked for a lot of signs.) Today I was asking for God to show me yellow roses, if we were going to win in our upcoming court hearing.

Outside the weather was blasting the midwestern winter cold. I knew that my yellow rose bush outside could not possibly offer a sudden bloom, due to the time of year. So I was fairly certain that if I was going to be seeing yellow roses, that they would absolutely be in answer to my sign request.

Although my sweet second husband brought me flowers every month on the day of our wedding anniversary for the first year we were married, I knew it highly unlikely that I would receive yellow roses from him, as it wasn't our day. We were experiencing the dead of winter, and yellow roses were hard to come by in our area, even from a florist's shop.

I happened to leave work early that day, for a doctor's appointment, and afterwards, I returned home. I sat down on my living room sofa, and turned on the television set to find a commercial playing that I had never seen before. The ad was for a used car dealership, one not operated locally. It was a really low budget commercial, one of those "Crazy Eddie" type of car dealerships, so it really got my attention. At the end of the commercial, the female announcer stood holding the largest bouquet of yellow roses I had ever seen. I quite obviously had the sign for the answer in which I was seeking.

* * *

I have found that the world of Spirit will use whatever means it has to, to get us the signs or confirmations that we ask, if we only open our hearts to look for and recognize them. I think its because I am so willing to accept what is being shown to me, and the fact that I have a spiritually open mind that I can easily see what others might choose to overlook. I am worthy of Spirit sending me a sign, and by golly, I will accept it when I see it, no matter what form it takes; and so should you.

In case you are still a nonbeliever in the power of asking for and receiving ethereal signs, let me tell you a few more signs that I asked for and received. You might be tempted to put these signs down as mere coincidences or some other explanation. But one thing I can tell you, is I have always tried to see through the eyes of my heart and not the eyes of my head, and that everything happens for a reason, signs included.

There are far too many so-called coincidences in life to be merely happenstance. I know that our lives are charted out before we arrive on the Earth plane, and everything that happens to us is all part of the overall plan for our lives. The coincidences or synchronicities are things that are planned for us to recognize Spiritual presences in our lives, helpers from the ethereal plane who are rooting for us to be successful in our life mission.

"I never get any signs," you might say to yourself. I firmly believe that we all receive signs and divine interventions, all throughout our lives. The difference between seeing signs or not seeing them lies within two fundamental principles.

One, we have to believe that we are worthy of receiving signs and blessings; and two, we have to open up our hearts to receive and accept them and not second guess the signs we actually do receive.

Another opportunity for the exhibition of divine signs came about for me while in the midst of the long months of the court trial. One evening just before bed, my new husband and I, together asked for a sign for each of us, to indicate that we would be successful with the current trial date's outcome. My hubby specifically requested that he be shown a checkered flag, which he figured not to be very common. I specifically asked for the sound of bells, knowing that I would not stand a chance in high heaven of hearing them, being housebound due to an illness at the time. That night we both went to sleep and the next morning, my husband went to work as per usual.

At two-thirty in the afternoon, (my typical sign time), I happened to glance out the living room window just in time to watch a single soap bubble float in the afternoon sun, in front of my house. The bubble glided along and then finally popped, directly in front of my view. "How odd," I said, looking out the window for the source of the soap bubble. I looked for children, but there were none around. I actually went outside onto my front porch, because I knew that the bubble had to have come from somewhere. But there were no children around at all. "Well, that's weird," I commented to myself out loud. I decided that the bubble had been put there just to get my attention, which it had, and I kept watch for my sign, which I felt would appear soon. I went to sit on the sofa, wondering from where the soap bubble could have originated, but something told me to leave the front door open so that I could hear through the screen door.

A minute or two later, I suddenly heard a tinkling sound. "What the devil is that?" I said, getting up from the sofa. I strained my ear to decipher the noise, and I suddenly determined it to be the sound of bells, like the kind you might find on a bicycle or a cart of some kind. The bells jingled and tinkled more loudly, and I decided to look outside, to locate the source of the sound.

Just as I peered out the screen door, I noticed a young boy, about fourteen or fifteen years old, pushing a hand cart, and on the top of the cart was a string of bells, creating the pleasant tinkling sound that I was clearly hearing.

We live in the city and I have seen vendors pushing hot dog carts at parades, or ice cream trucks going by, but I had never seen anyone pushing a small hand cart like this one, and certainly not this particular vendor in my neighborhood. The cart had writing on the side of it; written in another language, so I had no idea of what type of dessert or confection the boy might have been selling.

And yet here the young man was, clearly walking down the center of my street, at two-thirty in the afternoon on a weekday, selling something. To whom, I could not imagine, as most people were still in school or at work at that time of day. But here was my sign, in the form of bells on a pushcart, as I had requested. Incidentally, I never saw that young man before or since that day.

When my husband returned home from work that day, I told him about the boy with the pushcart and the bells that I had heard. He smiled and said, "of course you got your sign, want to hear about mine?" His eyes sparkled. "As soon as I got to work this morning, I went to the parts counter to see about a part for a customer. The counter man, who usually wears the same crummy shirt every single day to work, had a new T-shirt on today, and I happened to see what was printed on the front of it. It was a fifty-seven Chevy and it had a giant checkered flag across the front of it," he said, gleefully. "I knew right away that I had my sign," he said. "It was just too easy." It was the first time in my hubby's life that he had tried my sign request procedure and was absolutely stunned to discover that it actually worked.

* * *

Ask, and it shall be given you;
seek, and ye shall find;
knock, and it shall be opened unto you;

For every one that asketh receiveth;
and he that seeketh findeth;
and to him that knocketh it shall be opened.

– Matthew 7:7-8

ABBA SPEAKS

Whenever I have asked for a sign in my lifetime, I have always received one. It does not matter how we ask for a sign, but I have learned that it helps to be as specific as possible when asking for one. Be careful what you ask for, as the Spirit world is very precise in its responses.

Continuing on with the theme of the court hearings and the trial, I relied on whatever support I could get, either from loved ones here or in the hereafter. In my search for support, for a time, I spent some evenings reading and studying the Bible, which I had not done for many years.

During the evening, I had been watching television, flipping channels trying to find something to watch, to no avail. For some reason, I settled on a channel that had a comedian. I guess I reasoned that hearing something positive might lift my spirits. As soon as I settled on the channel however, the program went to commercial.

I watched a silly commercial where there were people dressed in costumes and performing on stage, as if at a rock concert. The folks were dressed in a style similar to the rock band ABBA, one of my favorite groups when I was growing up. The commercial was silly and had nothing to do with the band other than it was a spoof on the band to market a product. I thought very little more of it as I listened to several commercials in a row. I eventually grew tired waiting for the comedy show to return so I changed the channel once more.

I came across a movie in progress and decided I would watch a little bit of the movie and then go to bed. Strangely enough, as I watched, there appeared actresses who were upon a rock stage, dressed as the girls from the band ABBA again, and lip-synching to one of their hits. What was with the ABBA theme I wondered to myself? This was all too strange I thought, and I turned off the television for good. I decided to head off to bed lest I find a third show featuring ABBA that evening.

As I often did just before bed, I was reading and praying to God. I asked for the strength to get through the difficult court battle in the days to come. I prayed for God to help me accept the outcome of the trial, despite whatever verdict may arrive.

At the time, my ex-husband had alienated my young children and coerced them through gifts and promises of toys and vacations, to lie on his behalf and say that I was physically abusing them, so that he could gain custody. I cannot tell you how horrible it was to go through that part of life, but my family was apparently being put through it for some reason, and I could only guess at the time what spiritual lessons were to be learned from it. Despite the fact that I was completely innocent and my ex-husband had no witnesses or evidence, I did not trust how things were going to turn out in court, but I knew I desperately wanted the truth to come forth.

Just before finally drifting off to sleep, I found myself reading from the book of Matthew, in the New King James edition of the Bible. As I came across a verse that struck a chord with me, (it happened to be the third Abba reference I had received that evening!) I recited Matthew, 14:36 aloud. "Abba, Father, all things are possible through you. Take away this cup from me, nevertheless not what I will but what thou wilt." I asked God if I could be given the strength and fortitude to accept whatever He willed, whatever that might be for me and for my family, even if I did not necessarily agree with it. I went to sleep after completing my prayers.

At some point in the middle of the night, I awoke suddenly to find a very tall, very thin man standing right next to my bedside. For some reason his presence was not alarming to me. I thought I recognized him to be the image of my maternal grandfather, whose likeness I had seen only once before, in a photograph. The man had passed away long before I had been born, when my mother was very young.

As startling as it was to suddenly awaken and see him standing there, I was more impressed than frightened by what he said to me than by the fact that he was standing in the middle of my bedroom. He uttered one word to me before disappearing, and that one word was "Abba".

The word he spoke drew my complete attention and I felt immediately compelled to get up out of bed and go downstairs and look up the word "Abba" in the dictionary. I did not know why this man had appeared to me and what was the significance of his one word message, but I was sure I needed to find out.

Already aware that the word "Abba" meant God, I was led to read the entire definition from my dictionary. To my surprise, it also mentioned the Bible verse Matthew 14:36, which happened to be the exact same verse that I had repeated that night before retiring.

As I read the dictionary's definition, I felt a chill go down my back, as if I was reading a divine truth of some kind. I realized that the prayer I had prayed that night had been heard by those in Spirit, and I was being sent a message of hope and comfort from my deceased grandfather, from beyond.

* * *

Remember to always entertain strangers,
for in doing so,
you may be entertaining an Angel unawares.

– Hebrews 13:2

ANGEL LIGHTS

To me, one of the most intriguing signs that I occasionally experience are the presence of Angel lights. These are bright flashes of light that suddenly appear in our field of vision, and are not precipitated by positional changes, health problems or head injuries. The lights themselves resemble the round flashes of light I experienced as a child when my Mother would take our picture with her flash bulb camera. The flashes come and go for several seconds, sometimes up to a full minute; depending upon how open-minded we are to receiving them and the meaning of their purpose.

These flashes of light, which dance and blink before our eyes, are a blessing unto themselves and the divine way in which our Angels allow us to see their energy, alerting us to their presence in our lives.

I had seen these Angel lights many times before when I was younger, but I always thought they were a disturbance in vision. Perhaps I had low blood sugar or some sort of medical condition that caused them, I would reason.

After reading many books on the subject however, I happened to learn that I am not alone in my experiences of these phenomena; more people than I can count have had similar experiences in their own lives. So let me tell you about this encounter with the ethereal helpers in my life, and their own Angel lights.

After our first court trial was over with, and the unbelievable placement reversal verdict was rendered, my second husband and I went to visit our new attorney, who would be handling our immediate court appeal. Because of the manner in which our trial and case was handled, we felt we had an excellent appeal case and we were prepared to go the full mile in that regard. We knew that an appellate court should absolutely overturn the judgment that had been rendered not only unfairly, but egregiously and not without tremendous impropriety on the lower court's part.

My ex-husband, without any witnesses or evidence, and with only hearsay testimony unsupported by anyone except for himself, had successfully manipulated an entire court and its officers into believing that he deserved placement of our two minor children. It was even admitted that the children had lied about the abuse. It was also made clear that no abuse had occurred and the judge had even commented that my ex-husband had undoubtedly abused me while we were married. The judge's negativity toward me was simply that there might be an "air of tension" in our home. (Well of course there was, the dummies were trying to take away my children.)

A ruling had been reached on the basis of a comment the social worker had stated (her words were that we lived in a changing urban environment); and the children's court-appointed attorney who had done absolutely no investigative work. The judge ignored my witnesses who had testified truthfully, and also the children's counselors who indicated the children's admissions they had rehearsed their story in order to help their father win his court battle, at his insistence.

My children were ripped out of our loving, God-fearing two-parent family; away from their friends and school and six-years of excellent grades and given to a man who would lie and manipulate to get whatever he wanted. My children were now to live with him and a woman staying with him that was still married to a man living in another state. She had never even come to court nor had any investigative work been done on my ex-husband's home life to determine exactly what was in the children's best interests. Now I was supposed to allow the court to remove my children from my loving care, ignore their circumstances and simply accept it because there might be an air of tension in my home. Was everyone completely out of their mind? I wondered, enraged by the decision.

This had not been a fair trial by any stretch of the imagination. Because I lived outside of the county in which the case had been heard, I could only guess that to the judge and court officers, I was the equivalent of road kill. It was overly apparent that we had no legal rights in that family court, at least none that the other parties to this action wanted to acknowledge. We would have to appeal the decision and fight this thing, this ridiculous, can't-believe-they-actually-did-that court case, at whatever cost, to make it right.

There was no excuse for the family court to deliberately disregard the laws of the state, laws that were designed to protect me from having my children wrongfully removed from my care, without any legal basis whatsoever. But apparently part of my family's journey down here on this planet had deemed this process absolutely necessary for our Spiritual growth, because it was actually happening and there was nothing I could do to prevent it.

Some time after we got over the initial shock of the decision, my husband and I sought out a highly talented attorney who was also a court commissioner. He had actually sat upon the very same bench as the so-called judge in our case. This man knew well the laws of our state, and my husband and I gathered up any money we could find in order to hire him. We met and discussed our legal matters at length with our powerful new attorney, and were dismayed to find that our appeal process could easily take up to two years, far longer than what we should have been put through, but the appeal was our only option at that point.

If we did not fight this decision, not only would my family be completely destroyed, but also every family attorney that stood in that court room from that day forward could use the lower court's decision in our case, to change placement of children and rip innocent families apart for no reason other than where they lived geographically.

After our hour-long meeting, as we prepared to leave, my husband and I stood chatting with the attorney for a few moments. All of a sudden as I listened to my husband speaking with the attorney, I witnessed a large number of little round, very bright flashes of light dancing between the two men. There were about twenty or thirty of these flashes, and I was enjoying the feeling of peace they brought as well as the light show itself. I knew at once that the flashes I was seeing were from the Angels revealing themselves to me.

I felt very blessed for their appearance and I dared not interrupt the conversation between the two men, as I stood bearing witness to the divine helpers standing between them. The lights flashed gold, bronze and silver colors, and seemed to want to linger as long as necessary to prove them not merely a figment of my imagination. I even had a momentary doubt as to their existence, and thinking that my eyes were playing tricks on me, I looked away. But the lights did not follow in my field of vision.

Puzzled by what I was seeing, I resumed my glance at the two men and the lights were still present, and very actively flashing between them.

I took comfort in the lights more than usual, as I had recently asked God to send me a sign that my Angels were working in the background on this horrendous court case, in an effort to help us win not only because it was right, but also because the fundamental principles that the court had followed were discriminatory and dangerous.

I silently thanked God for the thoughtful proof of divine helpers in our lives, and I couldn't wait to tell my husband about the light show I had witnessed. As soon as we left the attorney's office, I excitedly started telling my hubby about the Angel lights I had seen. As soon as I stepped off the curb, I admit that I was so excited about what I had witnessed that my attentions were elsewhere and I did not look to see what was coming down the street.

Just as I stepped down, my husband, who happened to be looking at me as I was describing what I had seen, uttered a loud guttural sound. The noise struck me by surprise, and caused me to hesitate just long enough to miss being hit by the metro bus that soared past me, just a foot away. Had he not made that noise, I would have absolutely stepped in front of the bus, and been struck–and quite possibly killed.

Were the Angel lights there to save me from the bus? Possibly. Were they there for assurance that we were getting help from above on our court case? Probably. Why they were there was not important to me at all. The fact that they were there at all was the most important thing to me. I thanked both my husband and the Angels very graciously, for saving me from near catastrophe that afternoon. And I thanked God for allowing me to see my invisible but very active helpers.

I have seen Angel lights several times before in my life, usually when I was asking for proof that my Angels were real, that they were not just a figment of my imagination. It usually takes some time after I ask my Angels to reveal themselves before they actually will. It is almost as if they say "well, we'll show ourselves to you when we are ready, and not before."

But our Angels love us without question, and they will try to please us by showing themselves to us. They will allow us to see them through their Angel lights when we least expect them, when we are relaxed and mentally open to them. If our minds are open enough and they are certain that they will not scare us with their presence, they will reveal themselves openly, in whatever form we will most likely accept.

If we need them to show themselves in a human form, that is the form they will most likely take. If we can tolerate seeing them in a form with a glowing robe and wings, they will reveal themselves to us in that manner. Sometimes a simple sign or an object appearing out of nowhere or the most unlikely coincidences that occur in our lives at just the right moment, are proof positive that our Angels are around us.

Remember to always entertain strangers, for in doing so, you may be entertaining Angels unawares.

* * *

There are only two ways to live your life.
One is as though nothing is a miracle.
The other is as though everything is a miracle.

– Albert Einstein

HEAVENLY BIRTHDAY

There are many instances where electrical phenomena have occurred and people have believed the cause to be that of Spirit. I am certainly not alone in noticing that Spirit moves in ways in which we can understand. Some of those ways are in the form of interference with electrical currents, like turning on a light that is not plugged in, or ringing a doorbell when no one is at the door.

Since we are by biology, electrical beings, it is no surprise that Spirit would use the same process by which to communicate with us. One way that Spirit uses quite regularly to get a message through to me is through the flickering of lights or through the use of the telephone.

Although most of the time when we answer the phone and there is nothing but static on the other end, we simply hang up the phone and put the whole incident down to a wrong number or some other sort of anomaly. But what if it was Spirit trying to reach you, to communicate with you some form of a message?

Many of us have read stories about loved ones contacting them through the telephone during a time period when they could not possibly have done so, i.e. after they were dead. This should not be hard to believe knowing that the energy that is the soul component of our bodies is electrical in nature.

As I found myself turning forty years old, I was approaching the dreaded middle-age years. To tell the truth, I don't know if I was looking forward to reaching this landmark age or not. I do remember thinking how nice it would have been to have my father around for my fortieth birthday. Since he had been deceased at that time for eleven years, there was no way that he could have shared that day with me. Still, I wished to hear from my father. As I always lit a white candle in his honor for his birthday, I wondered if he would in turn, send me some sort of a happy birthday wish for this landmark year of mine.

I had been setting up a new home-based business and I had recently installed a new answering machine on the business phone line. I had some trouble with the answering machine and I was even considering removing it from the line, but finally decided I would leave well enough alone, just in case I received any phone calls while I was out.

The decision was probably a good one, because suddenly every single day, starting about a week before my fortieth birthday, there was a phone message left on the answering machine. That would not be strange to others, seeing as how I was operating a business out of my house. But what was strange was that I had just recently installed the phone line too, and no one had my business phone number—at least not yet.

Nevertheless, each day I was out taking care of errands, I returned home to see the blinking light of the answering machine innocently announcing that I had a phone message that needed listening to. So each day I pushed the "play" button on the machine to see who it was that had left me a message.

Each time I did this, I heard the following message. "3-3-7. If you'd like to make a call, please hang up and dial again." I never could ascertain the significance of the message, so I simply erased the call and mumbled something under my breath. And yet each day the episode would repeat itself. "3-3-7. If you'd like to make a call, please hang up and dial again."

Every day for six days (it occurred on a Saturday too) whenever I was out of the house, someone or something would call the business line and that was the message that would be left behind. Now you might think, okay, someone is trying to fax broadcast the phone number. I questioned why there was also a message left on a Saturday. One would think it not very likely that anyone would be working on a weekend. Furthermore, I left my home at various times of day, so the messages were not being left at the same time every day, either. To complicate the process, the phone never rang while I was at home, but rather only when I was out.

After a week of putting up with this weird activity, I finally let my husband in on the occurrences on the business line. "Maybe your father is just wishing you a happy birthday," said my husband, in a rather nonchalant way. "What do you mean?" I asked, doubtful. "Well," he said matter-of-factly, "three-three-seven. Maybe that is three plus thirty seven. Or thirty-three plus seven, or maybe three plus three plus seven which is four, and then nothing," he postulated. "Anyway you look at it, they all equal forty. So maybe your father is just trying to say happy birthday to you."

Happy birthday indeed. After my birthday, which was the very next day, a Sunday, the answering machine never "spoke" to me in that manner again.

* * *

The only true wisdom
is in knowing you know nothing.

– *Socrates*

NUMBERS AND DREAMS

I have been recording my dreams throughout my lifetime. For some reason I am blessed with a long transient stage between being completely asleep and becoming consciously awake. In this semi-conscious state, I am able to easily recall the dreams from the night before and quickly jot them down into my dream journal, which I keep by the bedside for those purposes.

I find that many of the dreams I record have much information contained within them. I do have a fair amount of prophetic dreams. Because of this, I often accurately predict earthquakes and other events, although I don't usually get the specifics of where or when they might occur, or even a time frame that could be useful to warn others of impending danger. Each time I receive these dreams, I know that within a few days to a week, the events will usually transpire.

I find one of the more interesting aspects of dream recording to be signs in the form of numbers or number combinations. Whenever numbers appear in my dreams, I will research their significance and attempt to apply their meaning to some aspect of my life. I find that numbers communicated to me via my dreams to be a relatively accurate method of Spirit communication for myself. Too bad however, that despite my requests, I never can get those lottery numbers!

In all seriousness, often my deceased loved ones will visit me during my sleep time, and give me messages or information that I could not possibly be aware of in my conscious hours. Upon verification, I find that the information they afford me to be quite accurate. When Spirit wants to communicate a message to me, one of the easiest methods for them to do so is by speaking to me directly during my sleep.

If you ever dream you have visited a loved one, then you probably have. In my dreams I have been happily dreaming about something else entirely when suddenly my grandmother will walk into the "room" and kindly announce that she has some numbers for me. Then she will say something like "4444". Okay, when I wake up I think to myself, what was that all about? But then I will look up the meaning of that particular number combination. For example, I find out that its meaning could be that the Angels are surrounding and help-ing me[3] or that the fours represent my own productivity, my efforts at organization, my drive for wholeness and my desire for global unity[4]. I would be completely unaware of the significance of the messages being sent to me if I did not look up the number combinations and apply them to my daily life. I fully recommend obtaining a dream interpretation book such as *Mary Summer Rain's Guide to Dream Symbols*[5].

Although not every symbol in our dreams has a practical meaning, some symbols may stand out as more important than others. Especially if you find yourself having a recurring dream and you can't decipher the meaning of the metaphors or symbols in your dream.

It may help to do some research into your dream symbols to help define their importance in your life. Keep in mind that books to deci-pher dream symbols are a tool; and the methods by which you apply their meanings are subjective to your own experiences. You have to use your own judgment to decipher the meanings in your own life. In other words, one symbol may mean one thing to one person and some-thing else entirely to the next person.

At any rate a book can help suggest practical meanings you may otherwise not discover yourself. Ultimately whatever rings true for you is the correct meaning for your symbol. Only you can decipher the metaphors in your dreams.

I have also experienced my deceased father visiting me in my dreams. I suppose from time to time he wishes that I see how he might be faring. Or perhaps it is he who wishes to check up on my progress in this life. Either way, I might see him playing football with some of his friends from his old neighborhood, although he appears much younger and healthier to me in the dream state than I ever remember him being while alive on this earth.

Similarly, I wished one evening to know how my grandmother was doing in the other dimension so I said a prayer to God asking that I be allowed to have a visit with her, so as to put my concerns to rest. Happily, I can share with you that I was allowed a brief visit with her that evening. In my dream, she was sitting with some of the ladies from her senior center, none of whom I had ever seen before, and they were knitting and sharing stories about their loved ones. Grandma spoke to me in the dream, "Oh, look who's come to see me. Why are you here?"

she asked, apparently surprised by my sudden presence.

Despite her curiosity to the reason for my visit, she seemed to welcome it, but I got the impression that she felt that she had left me just moments before, not that years had passed since she had last seen me.

"I just wanted to know if you are okay grandma." She smiled warmly at me, patted my hand and then replied, "Of course I am okay, we are all okay over here. No need to worry." With that I awoke, although I must say that I not only felt comfortable with where she was, but I actually felt like I had visited her in person. The colors in my dream had been so real and everything there was multi-dimensional.

When you have dreams that involve color, or sights or sounds that feel real to you, then you are probably actually visiting another dimension. Just keep that in mind when you go to bed at night. There is the probability that while our bodies are resting, our souls are traveling to other realms, continuing our spiritual journey while our bodies slumber peacefully below.

Watch also for number combinations appearing in your life. For example, animal and nature signs typically reveal themselves to me in the number combination of three. Everyone resonates to a different number sequence. You may find yourself seeing things in fours or sevens, or twos for example. We are all unique and we all have a unique vibration. My vibration as it happens to, tends to frequently manifest the number three.

While traveling down the highway with my second husband, I was having a half-hearted conversation about the possibility of losing my children through the errors of the family court.

As soon as I finished the conversation, I witnessed three cranes walking along the side of the highway. "How unusual," I thought to myself, as this stretch of highway was not known for much wildlife, let alone cranes. However, I pondered the meaning of the cranes and applied them to the conversation at hand. I suggested to myself that the cranes represented my two children and myself traveling through the court process.

A few minutes later my husband and I were discussing my ex-husband and his ridiculous lies that he had told while under oath. No sooner had we discussed that notion than I witnessed another crane. But this time the crane was standing in the field, along with a bunch of geese. "Look at that," I said to my husband. "A crane right there in the middle of a bunch of silly geese." I could see the truth in what I said as soon as I said it. My ex-husband was a silly goose. In other words, the universe was well aware of his deception and was making a concerted effort to help point out that fact to me.

I will often get other animal signs, usually in groups of three. Three crows, three deer, three turkeys, three woodpeckers, you get the idea. In Ted Andrews's books, *Animal Speak*[6], and *Animal-Wise*[7], he explores the significance of animals as spiritual totems. I urge you to explore the nature of animal signs and their important significance in our daily lives. Through their appearance in our life, they serve and protect, and offer unwavering guidance to us that we only have to accept to understand.

* * *

For the things which are seen are temporary,
but the things which are unseen are eternal

– 2 Corinthians 4:18

TIGER'S LEGACY

I have adopted many animals in life, one of many was an ex-racing greyhound named Tiger. Tiger was the gentlest soul of all creatures I have ever encountered.

Tiger was a good friend to me and followed me everywhere I went. I never felt alone when he was with me, and he helped me through the rough period of my life immediately following my divorce. I adopted him when he was retired from racing, at age five. For most of his adult life, he was in relatively good health. He enjoyed romping on the nearly six acres of land where we lived, and I found myself laughing more than I ordinarily would have, at his playful antics.

When Tiger was nearly twelve years old, he suddenly began limping. I noticed several times that his legs failed him completely for no apparent reason. A trip to the veterinarian's office confirmed my worst fears, and he was diagnosed with advanced osteosarcoma, bone cancer; a common affliction in older racing greyhounds.

The news was stunning and I hardly had time to digest it when the vet suggested that due to the disease's rapid progression, that my beloved friend would at best, have weeks to live. "Weeks?" I tried to grasp the meaning of the implications of the diagnosis. I knew the news would hit my children hard, as Tiger was their very first dog and he had become an integral part of our family.

The vet and I planned to provide Tiger with as comfortable an existence as possible, knowing full well that Tiger had so little time left. I hoped that once we got home, I could buy Tiger enough time so that my children could say goodbye to him in whatever manner they needed.

At the time, the children were traveling back and forth between my ex's house and my home, due to our visitation schedule. As it was, they could only visit Tiger three weekends per month. When Tiger was diagnosed, the children would not be around for two more weeks, and I pleaded with the powers that be for Tiger to live long enough so that they could spend some precious few days together.

As luck would have it, (or perhaps by divine intervention), Tiger did hang on for a few weeks. The children were told as gently as possible about Tiger's fate, and they understandably took the news hard. We spent the next two weekends coaxing Tiger to be videotaped while he performed basic tasks like eating, sleeping, walking around, barking and even eliminating; whatever the children needed. When they left the second weekend in a row, it was apparent to all that Tiger's time was finally drawing to a close.

My hubby and I had decided on euthanasia due to the quality of life Tiger now lacked. The pain, the drugs, his inability to eat, walk and such all played a key role in our decision. I tossed the decision around many times before conceding that it was the right thing to do for my friend. I remembered my dog Barney's struggle with cancer. Tiger was indeed suffering so we decided it was time for him to be at peace.

After taking him to the vet for the procedure, we returned home devastated at the loss of our friend. As I fought back my tears and hung my winter coat in the closet, I suddenly felt the unmistakable presence of my doggie friend standing right behind me, wagging his tail and smiling that big doggie smile of his. Startled, I turned rapidly around, only to find absolutely nothing behind me. But somehow I sensed Tiger standing there, and trying to communicate to me "I'm okay mom, I really am and I feel great!" The energy of Tiger was that of elation and joy, and not the sad, painful cancer-filled friend I had just left behind only a half hour before.

His invisible soul had stopped in long enough to communicate to me that he was Home and was healthy and happy once more. To show his gratitude for our loving commitment to him during his life, Tiger returned to me a gift of the knowledge that he was indeed right behind me, living on happily in Spirit.

* * *

I know God will not give me anything I can't handle.
I just wish He didn't trust me so much.

– Mother Teresa

THE HEALING

After a childhood of abuse, several abusive relationships, a divorce from a horrible husband, legal and financial difficulties and the loss of not one but two jobs, I was at a new low in the self-esteem department. I also was going through physical therapy for a work-related injury, and was involved in legal nightmares ranging from a malpractice suit, custody problems, a suit for worker's compensation, unemployment, and a mountain of bills left over from my divorce.

I had also been undergoing treatment for a heart arrhythmia caused by undiagnosed lyme disease that was being exacerbated by all of the stress. I never felt well any more, and between the injury, my heart, and everything else, I was losing hope that things would ever get better in my life. I truly felt that I was not going to live much longer and suffered from anxiety attacks from anything and everything. I was becoming a prisoner in my own mind.

Although I had recently remarried an exceptionally quiet and nice man, I still had a substantial amount of anger, bitterness, and depression with which I felt overburdened. I felt myself being crushed emotionally and spiritually from the weight of a lifetime of grief and suffering. I do not believe I had ever felt as low as I did that night, in April of 2001.

All of that baggage, combined with the recent loss of my beloved grandmother, whom I had missed an opportunity to see prior to her death, seemed more than enough to bear when a best friend stopped over to announce she was moving suddenly out of town. I felt abandoned by her and everyone else when I went to bed that evening. When I prayed to God as I did every evening, I cried. I hurt so much that I sobbed uncontrollably. An anguished cry that came from the depths of my soul told of the suffering I had endured many of the days of my life.

I begged God to heal me and relieve me of the burdens I was carrying, as I could no longer get out of bed each day. I was so tired that I wished for some way to magically leave this world. I did not have enough energy inside of me, neither for my new husband, nor for my children, and I honestly did not care if I saw the following day or not. Not knowing what else I could possibly do, I put myself into God's loving hands.

As I was getting into bed, I suddenly felt the presence of my beloved grandmother. Since I am a spiritual person, it did not frighten me in the least. I simply and casually said "Hi grandma," to the energy in the room and put myself to bed. I felt that grandma had somehow stopped in to visit me and I appreciated her visit although it offered me precious little comfort at the time.

A little while later my husband joined me and we both went to sleep. In the middle of the night, a vibration that shook the entire bed awakened me. I noticed that my body was vibrating at the same rate as the bed. In fact, it was then that I noticed that my body was actually causing the bed's vibration. It was a strange, rapid vibration and it permeated my entire being. I knew I was awake and even said my husband's name in an effort to get his attention, all the while remaining relaxed but definitely still vibrating. Unfortunately for me, my hubby was sound asleep and would not bear witness to the spectacle.

I peered through the darkness of the room and saw nothing at first. Then suddenly I saw a white oval glowing form at the foot of my bed. Unafraid, I watched it move to my right and come around to my side of the bed, all the while it expanded in height. I first saw a blur, then clearly, the outline of a beautiful Angel face and then wings, then a body. As the light moved toward me it unfolded and expanded to reveal an eight-foot tall male Angel (the bedroom had high ceilings).

He was beautifully robed in white, with creamy beige skin, short golden brown hair, and had a white sash about his waist. I could not see his feet but I was awestruck by the energy force that surrounded him. I felt immediately protected and loved, but at the same time, felt that he was a powerful force with whom not to be trifled. The power he emanated was indescribable. Though he did not speak, I knew instantly that he was my Guardian Angel, since there seemed to be some kind of a personal connection between us.

I turned my head, still feeling no fear, and heard the beating of bird wings. I then saw that the beating of wings was due to a large white dove that suddenly revealed itself to me and was now hovering directly above my chest. His eyes had beautiful red rubies in them and I saw tongues of fire inside the rubies. I lay silently observing these spectacles, and yet felt calm and peaceful.

As His wings beat over me in synch with the strange vibration, I received the knowledge that He was the Holy Spirit and He was there to heal me. I felt the outpouring of such love, peace, forgiveness and healing that was so totally overwhelming and so completely boundless that it filled every aspect of my soul.

During the experience, although my body was most assuredly lying upon my bed, the essence of my soul and what I can only describe as a duplicate energy body that was an exact copy of my physical body was instantly propelled into another dimension, beyond, yet somehow superimposed upon this dimension.

All the while the dove worked, it was communicated to me mentally that all the answers to every question I could ever ask were available in this other dimension. I did not ask any questions, but the knowledge was relayed to me that everything I could ever ask was somehow simply floating around in the space of the dimension where I was visiting, readily available. The knowledge was in the form of an energy field, and that energy field, I was told, could be tapped in small quantities, from within the earth realm. It was also relayed to me that the divine purpose for our existence is simply, to love.

There are no words in any language that can accurately describe the infinite power of the love of God. I knew in a moment that the Holy Spirit, Allah, Jesus, God, and any other words we humans use to describe the Entity known as our Creator, were all one and the same. Every human, animal, plant, rock, etc. on this world and on other worlds beyond are all part of a larger Unity, a "Oneness" that our tiny brains can only attempt to fathom.

Within this dimension, there was also no perception of time, as I knew it to be. No past, nor future, just the *now*. Everything in the universe was physically connected and it was really all very simple. We are all an energy vibration, all the way down to our cellular level, and everything resonates to its own vibration or frequency. The more we loved, the lighter and higher our frequency of vibration would become, and conversely, the less we loved, the lower and heavier we would become. God is the highest vibration in the universe and yet He is beyond what we perceive as our universe. He is the force that is everything both within and beyond at the same time.

As the dove hovered, it used its beak to remove a silver inch-thick cord from my heart. I saw the strange cord and guessed it to be several feet long. Somehow I knew there to be great power in this cord, and it was impressed upon me that I remain still for the procedure. He swallowed each section of the cord as He continued to remove it from my chest. This removal process lasted for about ten seconds and once it had ended, the dove hovered over my face to just above my mouth. Without any instructions, and in an almost robot-like manner, my lips automatically parted. He proceeded to replace the old cord with a new one. I watched as the new cord exited the bird's mouth and entered into my own. He was replacing that which He had removed and somehow this new cord was cleaner, better, or somehow different than that which He had previously removed.

As this was happening, my attentions turned again toward the Angel, who was now standing next to me, and he clasped his hands and said a silent prayer. He blessed himself after he was done and took a few steps backwards. I felt that he was praying that the gift I was being given would be accepted by me. I also felt that I was being given a gift and a job or task to do, although at the time, I was not consciously aware of what that task would be. But I was left with an impression that there was an important task or tasks for me to perform in my life, if I so chose to accept them.

It appeared that the dove had now finished, and I glanced at the Angel again. The dove disappeared and the Angel was now leaving in a similar manner to how he had arrived, in the ball of light. When the light reached the end of my bed, I saw a beautiful mosaic picture of the head of what I had been taught was Jesus, then the mosaic morphed into a robed depiction of the body of Jesus. His image proceeded to glide down my upstairs hallway, and descended the second floor stairway. I watched in awe as His reflection momentarily passed the window of the stairway, and a warm glow of light surrounded the image as it left.

When it was over, the vibration stopped and I immediately sat up in the bed, trying to awaken my sleeping husband. "Did you see that, did you see that? He was as tall as the ceiling! It was an Angel!" I said to my oblivious hubby, but nothing I did seemed to arouse him from his sleep. Excited but exhausted, I simply marveled at the experience for a while and lay down again. I found it difficult to contain my excitement at what had just happened, so it took a while for me to return to my slumber.

The next morning, as soon as I awoke, before I moved, I noticed that I felt like I weighed two thousand pounds. But as soon as I moved, my body was no longer heavy. Instead, it felt lighter than I had felt in years. I was not merely happy, but ecstatic. I felt so glad to be alive! I had no anger, bitterness, self-loathing, depression or anything else that was negative. I had been completely healed of any kind of negativity–to me, it was a miracle. I was so transformed by the experience that I could not even so much as dislike food that I previously had avoided because I did not enjoy eating it. The difference in me was dramatically noticeable and amazing.

My husband added to the authenticity of the experience in the morning when he reported to me that yes, he had felt the bed shaking that night. When I asked him if he had seen anything, he told me that although he had been awakened by the shaking of the bed, he felt someone tell him, "go back to sleep, this is for her," and so he had simply followed the directions he had been given. He seemed instinctively to know that I was being given a gift and he was not to interfere.

To further authenticate my experience, when I looked into the bathroom mirror that morning, where my forehead had been touched by the soft, beating wing tips of the dove, there now appeared tiny red blotches on my skin. The marks were all the visual proof I needed that something had indeed happened to me that night. I had been given a very rare gift and I felt absolutely blessed by the experience. The healing presence of God in my life changed me so profoundly that it continues to affect me in a positive way, to this day.

* * *

I tell you the truth,
if you have faith as small as a mustard seed,
you can say to this mountain,
"Move from here to there" and it will move.

– Matthew 17:20

AN OPENED MIND

Ever since the Angel visit in my life, I rise and end each day with a prayer of thankfulness for just being alive. I am truly thankful for the bad days and the challenges I have to face from which I may learn valuable, although many times, painful lessons. I am thankful for my friends and family, even for the ones who give me so much trouble. I have a renewed outlook on life and I have learned to appreciate life much more deeply than I had in the past.

I ask for God's will to be my own and to show me what that will is each day. Even though I am still human and make mistakes, I know that God loves each one of us, and I continue to try to love as much as possible. I now look at the world in a completely different manner than that which I had done before.

There is a type of healing that comes from opening one's soul to the possibility that our Creator exists and that He loves us. We need to live life with love and forgiveness and the knowledge that Love is all that really matters. We need to let go of the past hurts and look to the future for healing. We need to prosper one another through charity and by giving from the heart. When we love, love is returned to us ten-fold. Love can be present in many forms, and there is love in everything around us.

When we learn that we are all interconnected, we will realize that we are one Spirit, one body, and one soul. All the plants, animals, rocks, trees, sky, water, people, the universe and everything else around us are all aspects of our Creator. We have been given the tremendous gift of life, and that is not just life on this planet. It is the life of a soul that continues to live onward.

Open your mind to the possibility that there is something that you are a part of that is much greater than you. Come together with others around you and work together to love and give service to one another. Whether that be a hug, a kind word of praise, a smile, caring touch, a gift of material goods, or the support of a family member or friend, you can make a difference in the lives of others. Each one of us matters. We are each here to complete our journey, but we are here to work together, not as separate individuals, but together in unity of Spirit.

* * *

And ye shall know the truth
and the truth shall make you free.

– John 8:32

FINAL NOTE

I was watching television one afternoon following a discussion that I had just had with my second husband. As we ended our conversation, I had just repeated my recently adopted pet phrase to him; "the truth shall set you free." We had been discussing our current court appeals case and the fact that it would only be weeks now before the decision was rendered, hopefully in our favor. The truth would set us free, and set our family free. I mentally asked for confirmation from the Spirit world that we would be triumphant in court, after our long battle lasting several years.

I was watching *The Wayne Brady Show,* and the guest of the day happened to be another talk show host from the same network.

The guest was nearing the end of his interview with Wayne and I was catching the last moments of their discussion. Suddenly, I heard the guest say the words, "the truth shall set you free." Of course his words immediately caught my attention. What had led me to turn on the television set at the exact moment that I needed to hear the very words that had just been spoken? The man's exclamation was confirmation enough for me to understand that Spirit was speaking through him in order to get a message across to me.

Once again Spirit had attended to my needs and was echoing my words in the words of this celebrity, at the exact moment that I needed to hear them. It had not been a mere coincidence that I had turned on the television at that exact moment in time. Spirit wanted me to know that without a doubt, we would indeed be successful at the end of our long legal battle.

When you hear something that is clearly a message, whether you overhear a conversation, see a sign, or just hear words that somehow ring true to you, accept what you see and hear as the truth that it is. It is Spirit's way of communicating through subtle thoughts, words and signs. Spirit is speaking to each one of us, every day. It is solely up to us to receive Spirit's messages. When we open our hearts and ears to the sounds and signs of Spirit all around us, a wonderful thing begins to happen. Our perspective changes in every way. We no longer see the sun shining simply as the shining sun. We see the sun shining from within everything around us.

Spirit fills us from within, and guides us gently along the path that we are supposed to travel. We have helpers in the Spiritual realm who want us to succeed, to love, and to serve one another.

Listen to the signs all around you and open your heart to the ways of Spirit. Allow Spirit to move through you to affect others in a positive manner. pray, ask, receive.

Allow yourself to be blessed by Spirit. Don't analyze or deny that you are worthy. You are a worthy, powerful Spirit and you are a part of a larger whole. You are united with everyone and everything else around you. Spirit loves you and your Creator loves you. Never forget this fundamental truth. Spirit is truly *right behind you*, helping and communicating with us from beyond the Earth plane.

* * *

May Angels walk with you Always.

In Unity & Love,

– PJ Langhoff

BIBLIOGRAPHY

[1]*A Book of Angels*, by Sophie Burnham, (©1990, Ballantine Books/ Random House, New York, NY; and Random House of Canada Limited, Toronto Ontario, Canada)

[2]*Talking to Heaven*, by James Van Praagh, (©1997, Penguin Group, Putnam Inc., New York, NY)

[3]*Healing With the Angels*, by Doreen Virtue, (©1999, Hay House, Inc., Carlsbad, CA)

[4]*The Secret Language of Signs*, by Denise Linn, (©1996, Ballantine Books/Random House, New York, NY)

[5]*Mary Summer Rain's Guide to Dream Symbols*, by Mary Summer Rain and Alex Greystone, (©1996, Greystone Studio, Hampton Roads Publishing Co., Inc., Charlottsville, VA)

[6]*Animal Speak*, by Ted Andrews, (©1993, Llewellyn Publications, St. Paul, MN)

[7]*Animal-Wise*, by Ted Andrews, (©1999, Dragonhawk Publishing, Jackson, TN)

* * *

SUGGESTED READING

If you enjoyed this book and would like to find other books that also encompass Spirituality and related topics, may I suggest a few of my favorites:

She Talks With Angels, by Michelle Whitedove, (©2000, Whitedove Press, Fort Lauderdale, Florida)

Healing With The Angels, by Doreen Virtue, (©1999 Hay House, Inc. Carlsbad, CA)

Conversations With The Other Side, by Sylvia Browne, (©2002, Hay House, Inc., Carlsbad, California)

Driving Under The Influence Of Angels, by Jayne Howard Feldman, (©2002, A.R.E. Press, Virginia Beach, Virginia)

ABOUT THE AUTHOR

PJ Langhoff was born and raised in the American midwest. A fighter since birth, she has approached every situation with the same philosophy all her life. "I knew there had to be something better out there designed for my life than what I was living."

She faced abuse as a child and later, life on the street at age seventeen, bankruptcies, the loss of a child while pregnant, marital abuse and post-divorce custody problems lasting over ten years.

She contracted a chronic illness (lyme disease) at age thirty-one. The problems living with a debilitating illness only added to the difficult trials she would find herself thrown into at the hands of her ex-husband.

You can read about the many years of her family's unique custody struggles in her book, *Eyes of Pain*. It is a true story of how false accusations of child abuse and a faulty family court system destroyed one family's structure, but not its love.

Her goal for physical wellness over the course of more than a decade led to her founding a regional web site and support group for lyme patients and their families *(www.sewill.org),* and another national site for lyme patients which hosts their personal stories about lyme, *(Lyme League of America, www.lymeleague.com)*. She remains proactive in helping change attitudes and laws toward lyme patients at the grass-roots level.

Her experience with the many facets of this complex disease prompted her also to tell the story of lyme patients and the prejudices and difficulties they face regarding diagnosis and treatment, in her book, *The Singing Forest*.

Spiritual all her life, PJ relied on her strong psychic abilities and inner sense of self to overcome many of the challenges she faced, often without much support of family. She learned many early life lessons by negative example, always growing in the process and seeking a higher purpose spiritually.

She loves writing, antiques, music, design, riding and gardening. PJ volunteers for animal welfare organizations and spends time with her family of two children, and extended family of a variety of animals.

* * *

YOUR PERSONAL STORIES

The author is constructing a new book which will include stories about your true personal spiritual experiences. The book will include Angelic rescues; and miraculous or unexplained spiritual visitations or experiences. Near death experiences may also be included.

If you wish to share your story and participate in this project, please send your stories to the author at the address below. Due to space constraints, unfortunately not all stories will be published.

Only the first names of the parties submitting the stories will be published. You may include the city and state of your origin in your submission if you desire. Corporate names and the names of persons and/or businesses in your stories will be changed for privacy reasons.

Persons submitting stories must have the legal right to do so, and all rights to stories and their contents, in any form, become the sole property of PJ Langhoff. No other rights to the parties submitting are either expressed or implied.

Stories may be typed or neatly handwritten, or submitted on diskette or CD in Word. CDs or diskettes will not be returned.

Send stories to:
PJ Langhoff
Attn: Spirit Stories
PO Box 444
Hustisford, WI 53034   USA
Email: pj@avenuegrafx.com

The author wishes to express her gratitude for your interest in her projects.

Other books by PJ Langhoff
Coming soon or available now:

Walk Among Us; Lessons from our Spiritual Friends © 2006
A closer look at the Spiritual world around us

Wide River; Surviving life on a Spiritual Path © 2005
Surviving childhood abuse and gaining a spiritual perspective on life despite negativity

Eyes of Pain © 2006
False allegations of child abuse destroy one divorced family's structure but not its love

The Singing Forest, A Journey Through Lyme Disease © 2006
One woman's journey through Lyme disease, from diagnosis through treatment and self-discovery

Bread in a Can and Jewish Vikings © 2006
Lighthearted reflections on life in American suburbia

Please visit these important web sites:

Lyme League of America   *www.LymeLeague.com*
A site for Lyme patients and their families to register their names and location and post their personal stories about their struggles with this complex, misunderstood disease.

SE WI & IL Lyme Leagues   *www.Sewill.org*
A regional informational and support group web site for Lyme patients in the Midwest.

The Sunbear Squad   *www.Sunbearsquad.org*
An educational web site to raise awareness of animal abuse and neglect and how to report it responsibly.

Printed in the United States
105716LV00009B/220-237/A